Coming of Age

Coming of Age

Challenges and Opportunities in the 21st Century

Edited by Stuart J. Burgess

York 1999

ISBN-09536282-0-5
Published by Stuart J. Burgess

Produced by Outset Services Ltd, Boston Spa, West Yorkshire

To Leslie and Bernard,
companions on the journey
with affection

Contents

Foreword

The Rt Revd James Jones, Bishop of Liverpool

As we stand on the millennium bridge between the past and the future many are unsure whether the sun is setting or rising on our civilisation. The Christian has two responsibilities before God. The first is to look back and to remember what God has done in human history, for this memory helps to shape and to steer us into the future. The second is to look forward imaginatively and critically and to see how biblical principles can apply to situations that our faithful predecessors could never imagine. Like a person knotting together two ends of a rope the Christian is called to weave together faith and the future, the word and the world.

It gives me the greatest pleasure to commend this book to you which the Revd Stuart Burgess, President of the Methodist Conference for millennium year, has edited. Stuart and I worked together as friends and fellow ministers when I was Bishop of Hull and he Chairman of the York and Hull District. There, as well as here, he is a leader who pushes out the boundaries of the church. This book demonstrates his conviction that we should not limit the scope of the Kingdom of God within ecclesiastical fences. These essays begin to chart the territory of the future.

Nobody pretends that the map is clearly drawn yet. But these pages will prompt the reader to make their own contribution to shaping the future for Christ's sake and God's glory.

June 1999

Introduction

We live in a complex and fast changing society. For some people this is both interesting and exhilarating and for others sheer bewilderment. Many people may feel that the situation is so complex, past securities have almost disappeared and the only option is to retreat into safe ghettoes. I do not believe this is possible or desirable. It is my belief that the gospel, rooted in the incarnation and therefore proclaiming Jesus coming to this messy world, calls us to engage with the complexities of our world. The challenge is to listen to and engage with each other. To this end I hope this book facilitates discussion.

Any profits will be sent to Zambia to support two projects: 'Wider Horizons', which will help provide training opportunities for Student Ministers' families, and ZOCS, Zambian Open Community Schools, which exists to enable some of Zambia's most needy children to access basic quality education.

STUART J. BURGESS
President of the Methodist Conference
Southport, June 1999

The Internet: Coming to a Screen Near You!

Mark Bennett

FROM e-mail to e-commerce it all seems to have sprung up so quickly. Indeed the Internet is the fastest growing technology that history has ever seen. So fast in fact that no one really knows how many people are 'hooked-up', but a good estimate is around 150 million with that figure growing by 10% per month. That could mean 300 million people 'online' by the year 2000 and doubling again a year later, so that as many people will use the Internet as now use the phone. We have just reached the stage where the use of telephone lines for voice conversations has been overtaken by their use for exchanging data. Indeed the Chief Executive of one of the world's largest phone companies quite openly states that he has no idea what his corporation will look like in 10 years' time, nor who his competitors will be, nor what the business will be like. All that he is willing to admit is that 'something startling, intriguing and profound is afoot'.

The computer and the telephone have found each other and the result can only be described as a revolution. And when a revolution takes place no one stands on the sidelines: no spectators are allowed!

SO WHAT IS THE INTERNET?

Perhaps we can start with a practical example of what the Jones family are doing today.

Peter (7) is at school sharing e-mail messages (and some of his drawings) with 'keypals' in Surbiton, Sydney, Springfield or Singapore. Sarah (12) is researching for an assignment on 'African Music' by scanning the web (which is now the largest source of information in the world) for the best material — which may be in Africa or might well be in America — and then cutting and pasting it into her wordprocessor. In the evening Peter goes to the family's home computer and has a 'chat' with one of those same keypals in the USA, then plays an interactive game with them. Later on, using the same PC (after bedtime!), the children's mother, Janet, may spend an hour on the Internet taking part of the next module of her accountancy course and she is pleased with the report she finds from her tutor as well as the automatically marked exam results. Then her husband, Alan, takes over the keyboard and reads today's newspaper on the screen, pays some bills from his bank account, orders the week's shopping, and buys some books which will be delivered next day. Then he puts up a notice on his church's 'virtual' notice board about a special event at the harvest supper so that anyone 'online' in the town can read it.

The Joneses know that the Internet is simply a method of allowing computers from around the world to 'talk' to each other, and thus share messages and information. In fact it had its roots back in the days of the Cold War when it was designed to keep communications going in the event of a nuclear attack (and hence its robustness and ability to 're-route' messages when problems are sensed). However, it was quickly adopted by the academic community who realised its potential to assist with co-operative research work.

In just the last few years, however, its commercial potential has been realised, and now computers in almost every country in the world have access to 'the Net'. These computers may be in offices, schools, homes, libraries or anywhere where there is access to a phone line (or something more sophisticated like a fibre optic cable, as used for cable TV, or satellite or radio services). Personal Computers (PCs) can use normal home phone lines to become part of the Internet for sessions lasting from a few seconds to a few hours. Other PCs in offices or libraries may be permanently connected 24 hours a day.

At present the major use of the Internet remains the exchanging of electronic mail (e-mail), where messages typed on one computer are transferred to another (or a number of others) within a few seconds. E-mail addresses (like 'pjones@camberville.school.net.uk') are becoming as common as house addresses; and they can move with you. Replies can then be sent, documents shared and many more exchanges made than with normal ('snail') mail, and at a fraction of the cost. E-mail is more 'informal' than its conventional written counterpart and it is possible to correspond with people who you may never meet. More recently videoconferencing and directly interactive 'chat' sessions (where what one person types is seen on the screen of an individual or group of others scattered around the world) have become available too.

Coincident with the mass availability of PCs came the 'invention' of the world-wide web ('www'). This is a new way of presenting information on the Internet which makes it possible to relate topics using 'hypertext' links. Thus clicking on words in one document will present other documents with cross-related, and perhaps more detailed, information. Web 'browsers' have been developed which make information attractive and provide an integrated approach, so that it is not apparent whether what you see on your screen is coming from your own computer, another one in the same building, or one 15,000 miles away. All information the world over becomes interlinked.

What the Joneses are doing is becoming a commonplace. The use of the Internet doubles every 100 days. The number of web sites in July 1992 was 50; three years later it was 25,000; by mid-1998 4,500,000 and by the turn of the century it will have doubled again.

SO WHERE'S IT ALL HEADING?

The Internet is now a truly multi-media facility: it can carry sound and video as well as just words. With the advent of its commercialisation we are able to use it to do our shopping and provide our entertainment as well as improve our communications.

We can be sure that there will be a real push to ensure that as many people as possible have Internet access in order to exploit its commercial potential. The UK has a higher than average number of households with computers, at about 30%, but that still leaves a lot of homes without. However, this can quickly be solved by allowing people to use their existing TVs with appropriate adapter boxes, especially with the advent of digital television which is designed to encourage interaction.

Equally we need faster access speeds than can be provided by conventional telephone lines, which are fine for phone calls but not good for providing full-length videos. This problem is solved with new technologies and an increasing use of fibre cable and wireless signals. It will be just as easy to get access to the Internet when you are travelling as it will when you are at home or in the office.

So gradually existing media will merge, and the Internet will provide our voice, video, entertainment and information services. Then we will be able to choose exactly what we want to watch on TV and when we want to watch it; any programmes ever produced at any time in any sequence. The Internet will 'know' what our preferences are and our news, our entertainment, our shopping, our home learning, our information needs, will all be personalised to suit our tastes.

We should be able to move away from 'fixed' systems that look like the PCs or televisions that we know now to 'wearable' screens (attached like glasses) or large paper-thin screens attached to the walls. We will be able to use these to talk to anyone around the world (the Internet effectively removes any distinction in costs between communicating with someone in the next building or the next continent); to get up-to-the-minute news in any form; to move money; to study; to play; to relax; to find any information that we need (using intelligent search tools that will go looking for precisely what we want); to cast our votes in instant referenda; or to carry on our work, much more of which is likely to be done from home in the future.

AND WHERE AFTER THAT?

Current computers are very crude. Whatever the advertisers tell us, they still need reasonably high skill levels to operate them (albeit that young children seem to manage best of all!); they fail; and you need to be able to type — however slowly. Although they are improving all the time (and remember that PCs only really came onto the mass market in the mid-1980s when they seemed revolutionary) they have still to become truly easy to use.

But this is changing fast. There is a 'law' that predicates that computing power will double every 18 months. Since 1950 it has increased by a factor of over 10 billion. This power is now being used to build computers that operate using voice recognition and touch, thus obviating the need for typing. Within a very few years we should be able to talk to our computers around the home and they will be able to talk back to us. Once all our electrical equipment is also wired up together it will be possible to speak to the car on the way home so that it can switch on the microwave and have our supper ready for us. Or our houses will know to expect cold weather overnight (from a forecast received over the Internet) and adjust the heating automatically.

Whereas in the year 2000 a microchip might cost around 5p, this cost is likely to fall to 1p within 10 years. By then chips will be embedded in almost everything (just as we are seeing more computer power in a musical birthday card now than many offices in the 50s!). We will be able to wear chips (on earrings or tie clips) that will hold information about us that can pass to another person through a handshake. Our buildings will know where we are (from our body heat or radiated fields), how to react to us, what information to let us know, and even sense our mood. When we use the bathroom (and this is already 'happening' technology) the chips embedded there will be able to medically diagnose how we are feeling and, if anything is amiss, will be able to silently transmit that information to our doctor who will be able to let us know what to do.

Once microchips are a penny each (or whatever fraction of a Euro that is by then!) we will be able to embed them into paper. We will be able to write on them, allow the information to be recognised and transmitted to a computer and then we will be able to throw away the chip as we now throw away paper.

By 2020 we can expect to be moving towards a truly 'intelligent planet' where we are not merely storing data or information but turning it into knowledge. By then we can assume that the total sum of human experience will be available over the Internet; the collective knowledge of 5,000 years of recorded history. Thereafter too we can perhaps expect computers to begin to have some kind of 'feelings' themselves as we imbue them with a greater degree of artificial intelligence.

And if we think these are just pipedreams, remember how our grand parents might have felt about us flying around the world or watching things 5,000 miles away as they happen.

BUT WHAT ABOUT THE EFFECTS ON SOCIETY?

In the mid-15th century when Guttenburg invented the printing press there were only around 30,000 books in all Europe. Literacy and access to those books was a luxury, and a tool, of a tiny educated elite which jealously guarded such a precious resource. Within 50 years, however, Europe had over 9 million books and this mass availability stimulated the intellectual ferment needed for the Reformation and later the Renaissance. Will the mass availability of cheap and instant mass information that the Internet offers have the same kind of effect?

Many things will change, and among those already talked about are:

- The nature of 'news' will be different, for news will be available 24 hours a day on an instantaneous basis (filtered to show just the topics we are interested in). Everything is then happening 'all at once' around us (just as we can have constant music or constant humour piped to us now) and nothing will ever be news — in the sense of surprise — for we will already know it.
- The power relationship between the provider and the recipient of information will be reversed. Currently we read through a newspaper, or watch a TV programme, and information comes 'at us' in the sequential form that the provider intends. Once we have hypertext material available to us (as the web offers now) then we can jump about to exactly that material which interests us and move about from one provider to another as it suits us. The recipient is then 'in charge of' the information they receive.
- As a result of this, the recipient of information is no longer 'passive'. We can feed back our feelings towards the providers of entertainment, services and even government. Market forces may impel the first two to react in new ways, but government is also going to have to react very quickly (not something governments are normally noted for) and define new ways of interacting with its electorate. Whether this results in more 'knee jerk' reactions on the part of each party, or whether it results in truer democracy has yet to be seen. Being entertained and being enlightened are not always compatible.
- The move towards the 'global village' is happening very quickly (partly because the ending of the Cold War has meant that technologies have quickly become declassified), and we are having to adapt to new ways of

thinking and working at speeds quicker than ever experienced before. This globalisation includes the fact that we expect people everywhere to speak English (which is taking over as the language of the Internet) and to understand western cultural values.

- We are in an interesting situation where the younger generation is in the 'driving seat' of technological change in that they are growing up with it from day one and know how to cope with it. They are ready to adapt to and use the technology in a way that older generations are more likely to be excluded from.
- New forms of employment are emerging with a greater emphasis on 'knowledge workers' and a move away from more traditional skills. At the end of the day there will be the question of who is actually producing the wealth, and whether we can stop that wealth being personalised into the hands of a few people who have the 'right' skills.
- The 'virtual' community in which we might finish up living (which could be rich and rewarding) could also be one in which we have to change our interpersonal skills. We have to be very sure too that it is one that retains our essential spirituality.
- And, on a pessimistic note, we know too that the nature of war will change. We are already hearing about 'cyberwar' and billions of dollars are being moved into its prevention. Whole economies can be brought down over the Internet; individuals, companies and countries can be targeted, and society is going to have to rapidly develop another new series of skills to combat these forces (just as it is having to work towards coping with the 'millennium bug').

SOME FUNDAMENTAL QUESTIONS

In the last 100 years humankind has seen many new technologies appear, from telephones to cars to washing machines, and we have adapted our lives accordingly. Will the Internet just be absorbed into our lives in the same way? Some fundamental questions need asking, amongst which might be:

- Will everyone get a chance to be involved in such major changes, or will large sectors of the population be excluded? For example, of the 150 million with access to the Net at present about 90 million are in North America, 35 million in Europe, but only 1 million in Africa (and most of those in South Africa). Half the people in the world have never touched a telephone. The Internet has great potential to transform some developing economies and level the playing field a little, but who will ensure that it happens?

- And what about the elderly or the unemployed or illiterate? Are we liable to widen the 'knowledge gap' or can we bring them into the loop?
- Should everyone be expected to understand our language and cultural values? We cannot equate information with knowledge or wisdom that has been built up over generations. How can we learn and share the culture of others to enrich this new global 'mix'? And how can we learn about their faith, beliefs and understanding in a world of apparently increasing intolerance?
- With ever more information coming 'at us' it becomes increasingly difficult to differentiate hype from fact, or opinion from objectivity. How do we ensure that truth is maintained and that our democracy is built on well informed unbiased opinion, rather than being driven by market forces which may control the Internet just as they control much of our media? And how can we be sure that having 'too much' news does not drain us of all empathy with those in trouble?
- How do we ensure that our children grow up with sets of beliefs and values that we would like to share with them when they are part of such a rapidly changing culture? How can we allow them access to the technology without the danger of letting them loose in a new world where they may come across ideas for which they are not prepared? How do we teach them the new skills needed to deal with this when we ourselves may not be ready? We hope that new friendships will develop across physical borders, but how will that change the way we need to be? A very rapid process of education will be required, but how can we ensure it takes place?

The pessimist may argue that the new possibilities that the Internet brings could turn into mindless wall-to-wall pulp entertainment, which will leave us unable to think and at the mercy of the market.

The optimist will see the possibilities that relief from mundane tasks and the scope for sharing with others on a truly global scale will bring, including greater freedom and opportunities for progress. But that will mean some positive thinking, appropriate legislation, and not allowing progress to be dictated by wealthy technocrats.

WHAT ABOUT ME?

There is little doubt that the nature of economies will change; that human interaction will be different; and that our ways of learning and living will alter as a result of the Internet and whatever supersedes it. These are indeed exciting times.

And they have to be exciting times for the Church, but challenging ones too. A whole new way of interacting with people means that the Church needs to rethink its ways of presenting its message. Never before has it been possible to reach so many people so quickly. But there is no longer a passive audience for that message: 'interaction' is the by-word of the new society.

The Church has a vital role to play too in ensuring that it understands what is going on, technically, economically, socially, so that it is able to be at the forefront of those guiding legislation and encouraging participation; to ensure that this new opportunity is used for real *world* growth, and a growth in values and not just financial gain; that education is for all and not just a few; that the system is there for those who want to tell, as well as those who want to sell.

As Guttenburg, through a commercial invention, put the Bible into the hands of the people of the 15th century, we have to ask ourselves how we will use the new technologies to put the gospel for today into the hands of the generation of the 21st century, and how that technology can be used to deepen genuine fellowship. How can the 'still small voice' get heard in the ever filling ether?

QUESTIONS

Perhaps you might discuss some of the questions posed under 'Some Fundamental Questions' above, but also think about:

1 How can we as a church get to learn about the Internet and the opportunities and challenges that it presents us with?

2 What new opportunities for mission are likely to open up, and how can we ensure they are taken?

3 In what ways can we ensure that those who are already marginalised are not pushed further aside by new technology?

4 How can we use the new opportunities offered to us by access to better communications to share with those of different faiths?

5 What can your church do to reach out to a new generation which has learned to get its information in such a radically new way?

6 How can we ensure that the voice of God and the call to build God's Kingdom still reaches us over the increasing 'information overload'?

NB! Don't forget that the Methodist Church has its own web site at 'www.methodist.org.uk'.

Employment Prospects in the 21st Century

Harold S. Clark

THE LAST 100 YEARS

ANYONE in 1899 contemplating what work would be like in the next 100 years would have had some difficulty. Then, 20% of the working population worked on the land, today it is closer to 2% with a productivity which yields 100 times the output of 1900. The factors that have brought this about are technology and science applied to what we grow and how we grow food.

Many changes in urban work and life were brought about by the developing use of capital, some of them by people with strong Christian social principles. From highly casual arrangements where muscle power of horse and man were replaced by steam and the thoughts of lifelong careers, to the century end with new energy sources and short-term contracts as commonplace.

Battles between capital and labour have been a significant factor in the changes in working and living conditions. At the turn from the 19th to the 20th century Trade Unions and the labour movement were very weak. Some struggles had taken place in the earlier century of which the Tollpuddle Martyrs were the most famous, but there were others, many of them led by men with Christian convictions about the injustice under which their colleagues laboured. The 20th century has seen that phenomenal growth in democracy both in government and the workplace. With two world wars in the first half of the century strengthening the influence of labour the 50s and 60s saw Union power at its height and most antagonistic toward employers. By the end of the 70s and for the next 10 years and more, redundancy and unemployment emanating from a changing economy and a more robust body politic weakened the grip of the unions. Today we enjoy much more balanced industrial relations.

THE PRESENT

Looking forward from the present is equally difficult. Very few people in the developed world would contemplate writing with anything other than a computer but 10 years ago such things were a mystery to most. We are continually being made to think about developments in genetics, medicine, engineering and the like to such an extent that we cannot keep up. Environmental issues are a very real concern not only because of what we have done in the past (smoky chimneys, acid rain, global warming and nuclear residues) but what we might do to the earth and its environs in the future.

Amidst all of these uncertainties there are some realities. Very few people will work for one employer, or in one type of work, for the whole of their working life. What is required of us is flexibility and the security we once found in having a good job will be found in possessing the ability and willingness to learn new skills and in applying our 'old' knowledge in new ways.

The current growth in employment is in Call Centres. Multi floored buildings set in different parts of the country, or even the world, where for the price of a local phone call you can do all the banking you need to do, except physically put money in or physically get £5 notes out. Thousands of people answering phone calls that arrive at the automatic switchboard at the rate of hundreds per second. The employees of one large bank tell us that the busiest time they had was the morning of Princess Diana's death. Just think of the needs that we felt that day for someone to talk to and how much more accessible a banker at the end of a telephone was to those people.

It is well documented that today those with very special skills work very long hours, are much in demand and command high salaries. There are serious shortages of highly skilled engineers and technicians; the people who move scientific development into practical application and manufacture. The kind of jobs which get people out of trouble or the threat of it such as lawyers, doctors, accountants and consultants seem to be amongst the most stable at present. In another part of the economy it is almost impossible to find reliable tradespeople to look after the doors, the plumbing and the electricity, whilst at the same time we become more dependent upon the specialist. Who amongst ordinary people dare argue with the central heating engineer who tells us that the system needs flushing at £500, or with the automechanic who insists that the engine management chip needs replacing?

THE FUTURE OF WORK

It is not the first time this title has been used. Barrie Sherman and Clive Jenkins wrote a book with this title in the late 70s telling us of the changes needed in the economy and provision of work by the year 2000. Reviewing their conclusions they both could be dubbed prophets. The prophecies included: an increase of 5 million jobs needed, much improved childcare facilities essential, a flexible workforce capable of embracing the new technologies and much more accessible and appropriate training programmes. Some of these were dealt with successfully, others still need considerable attention. It is certainly true that we cannot rest in the quest to find purposeful jobs, particularly for the young and those from ethnic minorities.

EXPORTING JOBS

Much employment is no longer dependent upon heavy equipment in a particular location or upon pools of labour used to a particular type of manufacture. A result of this is the increasing ability of employers to export work around the globe at very short notice placing the labour of one part of the world in competition with that of all other parts of the world. It is not always easy to justify resistance to such moves when there is a desperate need to see other parts of the world develop. However, often the conditions under which employees are engaged in the third world are less than desirable. It may be necessary to see the development of international labour organisation to the level where it can challenge employers, some of whom have budgets and assets much larger than medium-sized nations.

COMMUNITY AND INDIVIDUAL

The level of difficulty in tackling these challenges lies in whether we have to deal with them on a macro level or as individuals. On a macro level politicians in national and local government and senior business people need to see the picture of Britain as a public company in which the stakeholders are the population. We are working directors of this company each adding to the wealth of it. The use of the word wealth is very important because it is not complete if we understand it as money alone. It means well-being. Therefore, those who are working within it for good order, good health, good education, and good care, not least home keepers, are contributing to the wealth of Britain PLC. What are the things they must do to identify the value and create the opportunity for people working in these areas to add to the well-being of the nation?

To make transition as painless as possible conditions must be right for people to be able to change job with the regularity needed. It then becomes the responsibility of society to make such provision so as to increase confidence and security. The factors which surround a change of job are many. Just a few are relocation, house, home, family (and their jobs), training, money, community, future job prospects for children and community.

STRESS OF FLEXIBILITY

As individuals how do we cope with the stresses associated with constantly changing jobs? If these changes are enforced, stress levels can be very high and motivation very low. Redundancy has been likened to bereavement where part of you is lost but life must go on. Sometimes the thought of another job is as unpalatable as contemplating a new partner after a recent loss. The difference being that a new job must be found and the sooner it is done the better it is for all. Callous? Maybe. Certainly it is emotionally hard.

If flexibility is the watchword for those seeking continuous employment then good information and training opportunities are important, as is the time to pursue them. In recent months we have seen significant changes in the way the Employment Services relate to job seekers but there needs to be much more from employers. That Service needs to expand to those who are still in employment, in partnership with their employers. They know that they will have need of people only for a short time in any particular task and it is crucial that they, with the help of government, permit and encourage personal career development of their people.

WHAT KIND OF WORK

It is almost impossible to predict the work that will be available in the next century, let alone the next millennium. There are two things that are certain. The first is that certain basic tasks will still have to be done. Many of the services concerned with personal presentation, hair and clothes, etc., will have to be done. It is part of human nature that those who can afford it will want more of that and other types of service. Human curiosity will demand that research and development will continue into new ways of using the earth's resources for the benefit of humanity. Capitalism will properly want to use its resource in manufacture and trade. Conservation and ecological concerns will generate a considerable amount of work and hopefully employment opportunities.

There is always the concern that very able and well motivated people will find employment and that there will always be some work for those willing to accept menial tasks, but the greatest problem is with those who occupy the middle ground who are by far the majority. Where will they find ways in which they can contribute to the common wealth of society? One of the areas we have not explored is the need for all of us to be human. This certainly includes responding to our economic needs but goes far beyond that as the people at the Banking Call Centre discovered the day Princess Diana died.

GOD'S INTENTION

No one can deny that God intended us to be economic animals. We need to sleep and eat. The world that God created demands that we work to satisfy our material needs and it is clear that God wants the best for his children and that can only be made available through work.

We can also rejoice in the fact that God considers us all to be his children, that is not to be confused with Karl Marx's equality for all, but seen in the context of a loving relationship with him and the others who surround us. Dealing with each other in this way is a highly complex and demanding thing for each of us. It demands much from personal discipleship, but how much more would it demand if we were to inject into this coming century the concepts implicit in belief in the Kingdom of God; establishing systems and organisations that take care of those left behind by the sharp requirements of the dynamism of new science and economy?

There could be many employment prospects in building humanity worthy of its creator if we could move the concept up the agenda of those with the capital to fund it.

QUESTIONS

1 What are the major changes in food production to be anticipated and how might they affect employment prospects in rural communities?

2 Are there any better prospects in the future for people in rural areas?

3 To resist the removal of work from our communities is to condemn the poor of other nations to more poverty. What is our personal response? ('Feed my sheep' 'In as much as you do it to one of these the least of my brothers, you do it to me')

4 What are the stresses involved in changing jobs and where can a Christian community help?

5 How do we ensure that all who contribute to the well-being of humanity are equally valued as Christ would want?

6 What can we do now to interpose the values of the Kingdom of God into working life?

An Environment of Responsibility — for the Environment

Arthur Fairhurst

IN the minds of many people 'environment' usually means the physical environment: global warming, climate change, air pollution, waste management, green belts or the regulation of transport and industry. The emphasis is negative and normally about damage and who is responsible. Specific issues receive detailed treatment when they hit the headlines, but insufficient attention is given to the fundamental factors which influence attitudes towards and concern for the physical environment. There is also a need to examine the nature of our corporate and individual responsibilities.

The 21st Report of the Royal Commission on Environmental Pollution grasps a nettle in recognising a trend that has been growing apace over the last two decades. In calling for a new approach to deciding environmental standards it affirms that our task is to prevent damage which may be global in scale and occur some time in the future. Whilst confirming the continuing need for rigorous and dispassionate analysis of issues there is also a plea for a much greater sensitivity towards people's values. Herein lies the challenge, not only to policy makers but for society in general. Perhaps the basic environmental issue is to create a sustainable 'environment of responsibility'.

Our understanding of and concern for the physical environment covers only a portion of the circumstances influencing our way of life. We have to be more aware of the broader environment and consider the social, political, and technical aspects in particular. Public concern, anxiety, uncertainty and insecurity are influenced by many factors not least the rapid pace of change and our perceived inability to influence the course of events. The physical environment is readily observed but the solutions to the problems we encounter lie elsewhere.

Since the end of the Cold War the rate of economic change, upwards and downwards, the globalisation of business competition and communications and the impact of IT have accelerated. Our political institutions, administration and social frameworks are under strain as a consequence because the response from society in general is not fast enough. We fail to recognise the implications of some technological developments until problems arise. Familiar reference points and long established standards are being swept away, leaving behind a moral vacuum. It is in this context that we are responding to current environmental threats. The controversies surrounding GM foods and the 'beef on the bone' response to the BSE threat are two recent examples along with our ever present concern about newer forms of industrial pollution. Potentially beneficial innovations are generating new social patterns but slower cultural responses are creating the problems. 24-hour shopping and Call Centres are but two examples. There is a serious mismatch between the pace of innovation and societal response. The response to threats to the physical environment has to involve both social and political responses, from Government, regulators, business and individuals in society.

The call for a continuing rigorous, dispassionate analysis and sensitivity to people's values has to be implemented in an atmosphere of mistrust and cynicism towards scientific expertise, political institutions and corporate power.

These attitudes will have to be modified through cultural, political and organisational changes. There is a worrying and unacceptable gulf between the scientific understanding of environmental issues on the one hand and public perceptions of the same issues on the other. Public perceptions are realities which have to be addressed. Science provides hard data and information but it is through political interpretation and the exercise of judgement that the limits of acceptability are determined. This process is not readily understood and controversy is thus fuelled. Furthermore, scientists and politicians can have different agendas and concerns. It is not difficult to understand why scientists, the public and politicians have different value systems. We have witnessed public outrage and genuine fear over GM food developments but despite the parliamentary posturing scientists view them as logical, reasonable and beneficial. The responses are consistent with the responsibilities and functions of those involved.

In order to take account of people's values judgements have to be made from the very beginning of investigations, not just when drawing conclusions. Much concern emanates from our different agendas, something which can be alleviated by achieving consensus on the definition of problems and determining acceptable limits to what is likely to be acceptable. Our well-established regulatory bodies have evolved from a very different environment where it was adequate and acceptable to examine issues on a case-by-case basis. In the current, fast changing environment, with wider interests and involvement, such an approach is increasingly impracticable. This is not a reflection on the competence of the people involved because they are dedicated professionals, it is a reflection on the systems of working and outdated protocol. Consensus is now required at the definition stage not when the reports are debated.

The Brent Spar disposal controversy was a striking example of how public, pressure groups, government and industry have different agendas and became involved at different stages. Shell and Government addressed the disposal of the rig in the context of the overall North Sea Oilfield operations. Their proposed solution met the prevailing legal and regulatory requirements. Greenpeace, and subsequently the public, viewed the issue as a case of using the oceans for the dumping of industrial waste, a much broader and emerging issue. The regulatory and legal regime was lagging behind the changes in societal values, attitudes and awareness. There was a real difference in the perceptions of the problem.

This is an area where beneficial and imaginary changes are urgently needed in order to embrace and accommodate genuine concerns, real or imagined, within the general public. Modernisation is a priority. The public has its own level of responsibility also and must seek to be more informed about issues rather than being over dependent on the output of pressure groups. Such institutional and cultural changes call for collaboration rather than confrontation, which in itself should reduce the level of unproductive time arising from a culture of contempt.

If lay concerns about future, broad environmental issues are dismissed as unfounded and irrational by politicians and experts, public mistrust will increase. The continuation of established practices, because they have worked in the past, is no longer a realistic option. The regulatory and political approach must take account of the changes in societal values and our physical environment. Wider consultation is an essential step in the process of restoring trust and confidence between public and authorities. The Government contribution to an environment of responsibility should include the establishment of broad-based consultative bodies involving industry, general public, NGOs, regulators and the scientific community. Such multi-disciplinary groups should be better able to recognise the concerns about the widening scale of environmental impacts. Scientific and technical interests must accommodate public sensibilities to define the broad limits of what is likely to be socially acceptable.

Trial and error will eventually produce the most effective consultative system but success will always be dependent on the exercise of mutual responsibility.

Participants will inevitably have their own agenda, expertise, experience and level of awareness which, over time, should combine to produce a consensus of understanding. Hopefully, we can bring about a better understanding of the limitations of science and an acknowledgement that uncertainty and unpredictability are facts of life that we have to take on board.

We have witnessed many environmental debates in Parliament and noted how the issues have become entangled in party political tactics. Until our parliamentary culture changes we shall have to be aware of the risks and learn to understand the rules of the 'Westminster Game'. Measures taken will no doubt continue to be regarded as overkill by some and inadequate by others. It is important that we recognise the different contributions made by our legislators and by our regulators in Whitehall and elsewhere.

Business has an important contribution to make to the climate of responsibility, if only to recognise and respond to the changes in public attitudes to corporate power. Many businesses are placing greater emphasis on and acknowledging the importance of communication with the general public as well as with customers, suppliers and shareholders. It has become necessary to keep promoting the benefits from its operations and to demonstrate its responsible attitudes to the neighbouring community and the environment in general. This does not mean that there is no adverse impact on the environment but that any impact is recognised, controlled and minimised. The Chemical Industries Association 'Responsible Care' programme is an excellent example of communication.

Over the last generation attitudes to business have changed markedly. In the past businesses were automatically assumed to deliver benefits and their 'right' to operate was determined by compliance with the law and the applicable regulations. Perhaps the decline in manufacturing activity and the present ascendancy of service industries has influenced present attitudes, but nowadays a well publicised 'good neighbour' policy is an essential part of the licence to operate. It should however be noted that many leading companies have had such a policy and approach for very many years. What was once optional is now essential. The 90s demand transparency, openness and accountability as general principles. Decisions are questioned if they are perceived to adversely affect our quality of life and threaten our environment. The distinctive shift has been away from 'benefits' toward 'risks' and the reasons for this shift should be explored.

Technological innovations have been both frequent and considerable, so much so that the benefits have been absorbed and taken for granted. Scientific developments, particularly related to analytical techniques, now enable us to measure and detect threats hitherto unknown and unimaginable. Scientists and regulators are able to measure and assess risks with greater precision enabling 'safer' business decisions to be made. The general public, however, is less concerned about the probability of things going wrong than with the consequences if things do go wrong. This failure to understand the quantified risk assessment should not be ignored. Lay people are concerned about what may happen to them, rather than the likelihood of something happening. The anxiety and insecurity thus arising adversely affects attitudes to the business and activity involved. Personal experience, values and beliefs dominate feelings about risk. These emotive responses are difficult to consolidate with the increasing precision and rigour of most technical investigations. The overriding desire is to retain a measure of control over what affects our lives. In an atmosphere of uncertainty about the consequences of new innovations a natural reaction is to opt for zero risk and resist the change. It is not a very realistic option.

Dialogue between business and community is now more commonplace but convincing the public of the acceptability of sensitive or critical decisions is still difficult. Compliance with the law and regulations no longer inspires public confidence because our legal frameworks are based largely on case law and the process therefore follows rather than anticipates technological and social change. Attitudes to business and of business are thus significantly influenced by the overall confidence in the regulatory bodies that police and enforce standards. This is a further reason why our regulatory systems need overhaul and updating.

No matter how successful a company might be in communicating and establishing good relations with its local community this cannot be effective in isolation. Sound decision-making through improved knowledge and scientific rigour is difficult to marry with social concerns unless there is an independent, acceptable, authoritative framework of reference. Questions about the extent to which companies should maintain an awareness of changes in societal values are valid. The responsibility of government to incorporate such awareness into our political frameworks is another. The environment of responsibility requires a tripartite response — Government, business and society, through broad representation.

In considering our individual responses the starting point must be the ambivalent attitude towards what we perceive to be environmentally sensitive activity. It is a truism that 'with public sentiment nothing can fail; without it nothing can succeed'. Many businesses are in danger of losing the communication battle for the public mind. We have come to regard the benefits as a right but without considering the balancing costs and risks. An aspect of our individual responsibility, in the application of value judgements, is to balance the benefits against the costs. Consider the Energy Industry, global warming and climate change. It is simply impossible to imagine today's society without energy, it is an absolute prerequisite for the economic fight against poverty, for social and economic progress. To understand the contribution of energy may for some become a simple analytical exercise but the question to answer is, how is it to be valued? There are two sides to any equation, both of which need to be valued. The environmental risks have to be weighed against the social and economic benefits in making our value and moral judgements.

Political judgements are involved when the quantified scientific and technical data are balanced against the social factors of acceptability. The 'precautionary principle' is applied. The politicians usually err on the safe side but when companies meet the public it often becomes apparent that there is little understanding of this aspect of our national policy making. The 'beef on the bone' controversy is a recent example.

A hindrance to a fuller and balanced understanding of the issues involved in scientific and technical controversy is the media hype and, to a lesser extent, the involvement of single issue pressure groups. When the media become involved the focus of attention changes, controversy is fuelled, positions become polarised, rights and wrongs are emphasised, values and principles are quoted and an attempt is made to apportion blame. It all makes for good entertainment but a dispassionate examination is made difficult if not impossible. Pressure groups will pursue their own agenda vigorously and differing interpretations quickly emerge. This was the case in the 'lead in petrol' debate of the early 80s. Some will oppose risk at any price, others will wish to take a more balanced position after weighing risks against benefits but the politicians and administrators find themselves as jam in the sandwich of social controversy. The prime risk is that the judgements made in such circumstances can be seriously flawed.

Government, regulators and business are challenged in such circumstances, motives are questioned, vested interest is suggested and higher profits are alleged to be the ultimate objective. Who will question the altruism of the media and the pressure groups? Who is in a position to do so? A former Minister of Higher Education put forward the view, in a private discussion, that the level of understanding of scientific principles among the general public was insufficient to enable them to challenge the media with any confidence. The counter question is how competent are the media to tackle complex scientific issues with authority? Is the standard of science education adequate for our modern society? Whatever our views may be, our responsibility for the environment should include vigorous questioning of the media and pressure groups in order to test the rigour of their case and arguments.

How are our individual concerns going to be met? Consultation, representation, greater knowledge and understanding, personal involvement are all well tried methods. We may follow the guidelines of good practice by greater use of public transport, by recycling our waste, reducing our energy consumption and avoiding the use of pesticides and herbicides in the garden. If our values and judgements are to be taken into account in environmental issues, how do we articulate and represent them? The recommendation of the Royal Commission provides society with the opportunity for involvement from the outset. To be informed and to inform others should be a guiding principle. The most convincing arguments will undoubtedly come from those who are well informed and experience indicates that such contributions will be welcomed by business and Parliament. Individual study, perusal of scientific and technical journals and use of the Internet are obvious ways of enhancing our knowledge. A greater knowledge and understanding will lead to more balanced judgements. The risk-benefit equation, assessment of the advantages and disadvantages and the implications of particular decisions and alternative options are essential facets of an informed and balanced debate. We need to be in a position to generate such debates at all levels of society. Representation to our MPs is a channel open to us all and one that is not used enough. The exercise of responsibility should be seen as part of our Christian stewardship but the level of involvement will vary according to ability and experience. The onus is on each of us to make a contribution.

A collaborative, inclusive, rather than combative, exclusive approach requires changes to our institutions and practices, but what about our values? How different are the value judgements of people in government, business and society in general? Do we each have different values in the various environments in which we find ourselves? How consistent should we be? Ultimately we rely on the judgements of people either collectively or as individuals.

The underlying aim of this contribution is to ask how we may combine our concerns for the physical environment through the exercise and application of responsibility in the various spheres in which we live and work. The change process has to apply through our culture but our responses have to be much sharper. There will inevitably be tensions as we strive for a wider consensus. In our multi-cultural, multi-faith society there is bound to be a whole range of attitudes and values relating to the environment. In such circumstances how do we each make our responsible contribution?

One can foresee a dynamic situation where a more informed environmental debate intensifies. There will be continuing campaigns to influence our values from groups and organisations with their own agenda. There must be a concerted effort by business, government and administrators to regain public trust and confidence and change attitudes. Perhaps the greater tension will arise as we try to accommodate the physical and social impact of further technological innovations which the majority deem to be acceptable. There is much to think about and to be concerned about as we broaden our environmental horizons.

QUESTIONS

1 Does our faith enable us to make a unique contribution to the environmental debate? If so, how? If not, why? Consider practical options open to the church.

2 Detail the influence of the various environments in which we find ourselves on our personal values. How does our experience at home, work,

in the community and as members of the church affect our concern for (a) the physical environment, (b) the wider environment in which we live?

3 Examine ways in which (a) individuals and (b) the church family may contribute to a greater understanding of the environmental issues facing businesses. What part can the church play in fostering closer links between industry and the community?

A Medical Opportunity — Theological and Ethical Questions

Julie Norris

IMAGINE that your heart was so diseased that you could no longer carry out the normal functions of life. You discover that your prognosis is poor unless you can receive a heart transplant. You are told that, whilst everything is being done to search, the chances of finding a suitable donor organ are not great. Then you hear that there is an organ available. Just as your hopes are beginning to rise you are told that this is a heart that has been taken from a pig. It is pointed out that pig heart valves have been used in heart surgery for some time and that this is a further development of the technology. You are just beginning to get your mind around the idea when a practical problem occurs to you. You have heard that it is not possible to transplant organs between species because the recipient body will reject the donor organ. Your surgeon tells you that the heart you will receive has come from a pig that has been genetically modified with a human gene to reduce the possibility of immunological rejection. If you could be reassured that there was a good chance of success, would you agree to this operation?

Scientists are currently researching into this possible application of biotechnology and hope to be able to offer it as a real possibility in the future.

Biotechnology is already a significant influence on our lives and is set to have greater influence in the future. There are many issues which arise for us as Christians faced with the scenario we have outlined above. Amongst these are the questions: How does this biotechnology affect our faith in God? How do we decide what is right? What do we have to contribute to the public debate about the future of biotechnology? Let us consider these in greater detail.

DOES BIOTECHNOLOGY IMPINGE ON OUR FAITH IN GOD?

There are those who say that understanding the genetic development of life removes any need to believe in God at all. Nature is adept at producing new life forms through genetic mutation. Any idea that God might have fixed, predetermined and completed creation at the beginning simply does not fit with our understanding of genes.

However, belief in God is not incompatible with what we are discovering about genes. It is possible to hold together a belief in genetic evolution and a belief in God as a loving and dynamic force within creation. Indeed, we could make a case that an understanding of God as Creator is the best explanation of why things are as they are. We need to try to understand how God initiates change and is involved in the evolutionary process. Christian theology has held that God is personally and lovingly involved in the activity of creation. We now understand this to mean that God is a force of love who created an incomplete but emerging world where there are new possibilities constantly arising. This point of view holds that God's work of creation is something which is ongoing and is an expression of God's own life and loving personality. God is, in this activity, constantly inviting creation to share God's work and life.

That we might be invited by God to become co-workers is a profound and transforming notion. For this is an invitation not just to share God's creative work, but to share God's very life. This would indicate that God actually wants us to be creatively involved in changing ourselves and our world for the better. If this is so then maybe it changes our attitude towards activity that has been considered to be 'playing God' and therefore inappropriate for us. If we accept that the world is emerging then all the decisions we make become more significant. We ask ourselves whether we will, by what we do, enable people to live more lovingly, more creatively and in less isolation? If we can do this by the careful use of biotechnology, then surely we would be wrong not to?

If we believe that God is Creator this inevitably leads us to value creation. Biotechnology can bring another dimension to this. As we understand more about the genetic structure of life we are made aware of our biological nature. We are members of a human species. This can bring insights into our connectedness with the rest of creation. For example, it has been discovered that we share many genetic features with chimpanzees. Awareness of this could serve to make us more conscious of the intrinsic value of other animals.

Some have suggested that biotechnology regards human beings rather like machines and leaves no room for faith or the freedom to choose what we are or will be. This view says that we are completely determined by our genes. In fact it is now understood that environmental factors are highly significant in determining whether or not a gene is 'switched on', whether or not a genetic predisposition becomes active. Of course our genes are significant in making us what we are, but so too is the environment in which we live and the experiences we have, as well as our memories. There is a complicated interplay among these which accounts for our individuality. This restores significance to our faith experiences. Science does not support the view that human beings are determined by their genes. So we are not forced, on this ground, to abandon the idea that we can make choices about the shape of our lives. Indeed, biotechnology gives us many more tools through which we can exercise our choices. It provides us with significant opportunities to consider freely the future of the human race.

The possibilities of biotechnology as a tool to benefit humankind are staggering and scary. There is the potential to use it creatively and the risk that it could cause harm. How can we decide what is the right and best use of biotechnology?

HOW DO WE DECIDE WHAT IS RIGHT?

Any idea that we can draw direct parallels from the Bible soon breaks down. Although the biblical and traditional texts have insights into God's loving involvement in creation, we cannot find clear moral arguments to support or reject biotechnology. Some Christians have argued that the moral imperatives are nonetheless clear; biotechnology is an inappropriate interference in nature. Here we have already challenged an anti-technological stance by suggesting that human beings may have a God-given moral invitation to be creatively involved in changing things for the better. Anti-technological arguments are unlikely to be persuasive precisely because they sacrifice possible benefits. But it would be a mistake to suppose that this gives us licence to be careless. We have to take seriously the possibility of harm and take steps to minimise risks.

Far from having a ready made ethical system which tells us what we should or should not do, we have to come to moral judgements on a case by case basis. The process of making the decision requires us to hold in play many different factors — such as, relevant scientific information, insights from our faith, legal constraints and risk assessment — until through reflection, conversation and prayer, we feel that we have reached an adequate understanding on which we can make a judgement. The process is complicated. It requires that we gain sufficient knowledge to be able to make a decision whether or not to proceed with a biotechnological application. When we make that decision, we do so because we are satisfied that it is right from all the different points of view.

As Christians we have something distinctive to bring to the conversation about what is an ethical and appropriate use of biotechnology. We bring belief in a loving God who initiates change and encourages us to do the same. We have a belief in the intrinsic value of creation. We have a biblical obligation to be concerned for the poor, vulnerable and the powerless. And we have an interest in shaping the future of society and bringing the Kingdom of God.

What ethical issues are raised by the particular scientific application which uses pigs which have been genetically modified with a human gene (or as they are sometimes called, transgenic pigs,) to produce hearts for human heart transplant surgery?

THE ETHICAL ISSUES OF TRANSGENIC PIGS USED IN HEART SURGERY

In trying to decide whether a particular medical application is ethical it has been argued that there is a moral distinction to be made between therapeutic and non-therapeutic technologies, and that only therapeutic applications should be carried out. Where we are talking about medical procedures this is a helpful suggestion, not only because it rules out selective breeding of humans and biological warfare, but also because it stresses the primacy of the individual over institutions and society. In the case which we are investigating the therapeutic goals of the procedures are clear.

The possibility of using pig hearts for human medicine raises the question whether it is appropriate to use animals for medical purposes. There are those who argue that to use animals for our own ends is a form of 'species-ism' and that there is no moral reason to justify using animals to service our needs. It is argued that this does not respect the animals' intrinsic value. It has also been suggested that this could take human beings down a slippery slope which would result in an outright disregard of all animal, and ultimately human, life with degrading results.

It is important to recognise that we have choices about whether or not we eat meat, or use animals in human medicine. There will always be some who would refuse treatments that make use of transgenic pig heart because of their opposition to this use of animals. However, there is some justification for a preference for human life over and against the life of an animal. We do value human life above the life of animals. This is more than simple empathy with our own species. We recognise the greater possibility of contributing to the well-being of others, making meaningful relationships and living a meaningful life, in the human life. The use of animals to save human life does not result in a devaluing of life. There seems to be good moral grounds for striving to ensure that animals are treated with appropriate respect and without cruelty. Bu the sacrifice of an animal in order to bring life to a human could fill us with gratitude and lead us to value highly both the pig and the enhanced life of the patient.

There are of course risks in using gene technology. It has been observed that the general public assesses risks differently from scientists. Often we have a strong gut-reaction to new technologies and are fearful of unknown consequences. Sometimes our intuitions persuade us that there is a serious ethical problem with the technology. But sometimes the feelings subside as we get used to the ideas. We need to understand why we feel as we do. We are helped in this if scientists provide us with reliable information about the risks and the benefits of technology. We also want to be reassured that the scientists have not concealed important facts because of their interests in the development of the technology.

Some of our anxieties about the use of genetically modified pigs can be assuaged. There seems to be little probability that we might create a monster pig, or that pig genes might inadvertently be absorbed into the genetic make-up of the recipient patient. But these are real fears that patients might express, and both of these need to be taken seriously and addressed by the medical profession.

Another area of great anxiety is whether or not pig viruses could inadvertently be introduced into a human being through the surgical use of pig organs. Scientists are still undecided about this, though we may note that heart valves, and other pig products, have been used in medicine for some time. However, our experience of the transference of BSE to humans suggests that there is need for great caution.

It is not yet clear what the prognosis would be for a patient after receiving such a transplanted pig heart. But, supposing that through this procedure human beings could be given a new lease of life, supposing that scientists could reassure us from actual research that there is little chance of passing a virus to us through these procedures, and supposing that the trials showed that there were minimal risks of inadvertently altering our own genetic structure by using the transgenically modified pig heart, what would you decide and why?

Finally it is worth remarking that there is currently a lack of social and legal structures to regulate and direct biotechnology. We want to ensure that large biotechnology companies are regulated for the benefit of society and are not simply pursuing their profit motive. At the moment companies involved in pioneering research are more willing to enter into debates with the general public because they fear public pressure could result in calls for a moratorium on their work. But this is not a satisfactory state of affairs. We need proper structures to ensure that the work of biotechnology is monitored and does shape a better future.

QUESTIONS

1 How do you think that biotechnology affects our faith in God?

2 What decision would you make about whether or not this particular procedure should be carried out and why?

3 Do you think that animals should be used to benefit human beings?

4 What sort of regulatory structures would make you more confident in biotechnology?

Forgiveness: Is it Possible?

Bernard Brady

INTRODUCTION

CHRISTIANITY, along with other religions, sees forgiveness as one of the central virtues, so central that in the New Testament it is seen as an essential condition of salvation. However, the world of analysis and psychotherapy has pointed out that the use of this virtue by Christian men and women can result in them using it as a cover, a pseudo-forgiving, using the psychological defences of splitting into one being all good or all bad, denial, and projecting of one's own painful feelings. A false understanding of forgiveness can lead to someone feeling that they must deny all aggressive feelings of hate and anger to the one who has offended them, a state of perfection which many feel to be impossible.

I would like to suggest that the capacity to forgive is necessary both for spiritual and psychological health and that this involves looking at the internal world of the mind as much as one's external world of relationships.

AN EXPERIENCE OF BEING UNFORGIVEN

V. J. Donovan's book, *Christianity Rediscovered* (1978) describes his visit to a Masai village where, speaking to the villagers, he noticed a man hovering on the outskirts of the crowd, clearly someone who was not accepted by the others. He spoke to the priest after the meeting to ask if the God of whom the priest spoke accepted those who had broken village taboos. The Masai have no word for forgiveness, so this man had no hope of ever being accepted. Life without forgiveness is dire.

A PSYCHOLOGICAL VIEW

When I introduced the idea of forgiveness in a psychotherapy training seminar I was struck by how the group divided into two camps, one which said it had no place in the world of therapy, the other which saw how it might fit in with the work of the therapist as he/she struggles to heal the hurts which clients bring. The latter group saw forgiveness as a defence which the client needed to give up. Certainly many therapists would be suspicious of the religious dimensions implied in the word. However, in doing a search of the psychological literature in 1995, it became clear that considerable attention has been paid to the concept of forgiveness since the mid-80s and how it can be seen as a helpful tool of the therapist in bringing about a deeper healing of past hurts.

Theologians and psychologists understand forgiveness in different ways. While the theologian links it with a relationship with God and others, the therapist is concerned with the intra-psychic process which may or may not have implications for others, especially the offender. In dealing with abused clients the question of forgiveness can be crucial. The client who says that they cannot ever forgive, or the one who says they have forgiven and forgotten, may both need the therapist's help, the former to look at how the hurt and pain are still there, the latter to look more closely behind the perceived forgiveness.

Forgiveness has a double aspect, one intra psychic, which involves the giving up of resentment and anger, the other interpersonal, which involves surrendering the claim to revenge and punishment. It is a word that can cover denial and repression, short circuiting the necessary stages of anger and resentment, creating a superficial forgiveness concealing the sometimes murderous hate.

In our efforts to seek peace of mind it is easy to project our pain and guilt on to the perceived offender. Unable to see them as whole people we tend to demonise them into personifications of evil, not recognising the distorted parts of ourselves in the process. While we condemn the cruelty of a Saddam or the punishment beatings of the paramilitaries, who is to say that they do not conveniently carry some of our own darker nature? When projections flourish both God and one's neighbour can become persecutory, and reality can become tenuous. Then the forgiving process cannot begin because one may not be in touch with a real person.

FORGIVENESS IS DIFFICULT

Being in touch with a real person involves a withdrawal of the images, fantasies and memories we have projected on to them. This process needs a change in our inner world and a knowing of ourselves. Behind the guilt of which we are so conscious there lies a deeper more powerful feeling which goes to the heart of how we see ourselves. The feeling of shame, although often confused with guilt, comes earlier, when our sense of self is more fragile. It is more about seeing ourselves as worthless than feeling guilty at what we may have done. Guilt is about fearing punishment and retaliation, while shame is our reaction to failure and loss of our ideas. We defend against shame with anger, blame, the assertion of being right, or with depression. While forgiveness is seen in relation to guilt, perhaps the forgiveness of self is a necessary pre-condition to forgiving the other.

Forgiveness is about changing our inner world which is made up of the images we have about ourselves and others and how they interrelate. If we fail to change our inner world then we do not achieve true forgiveness, but only a partial one. Theologians who are conscious of the present malaise in the practice of sacramental confession might well consider how detached the process can be and how the ritual can conceal an untouched inner attitude hostile to true forgiveness. If the past event is left with its power untouched then it is not surprising that the compulsion to repeat remains.

M. A. Coate in her book *Sin, Guilt and Forgiveness* writes of the power of ritual in private confession to help the penitent get in touch with their inner life. Religious imagery can touch powerful early feelings which may have been long buried, but perhaps the pastor needs to ponder that penitents need to have achieved a certain level of spiritual and psychological development before they may be in a position to use the sacrament. Others may need a holding and a containing so that they can relive their fears in a safe environment while they are psychologically unable to receive and give forgiveness. The more threatening are the internal bad memories, the worse is the sense of sin and the more persecuting can God appear to be. The guilt that results from this process is not the healthy guilt that leads to concern and the beginning of the forgiveness process, but rather an unhealthy guilt which fears punishment.

If forgiveness is about integrating the opposing feelings of love and hate, involving as it does the giving up of the right to revenge, then it runs counter to the basic human instinct for retaliation and retribution. When Scripture says that forgiveness is an essential condition of salvation then it is asking for a complex reality involving spiritual and psychological skill and development. The challenge to accept parts of the personality which have been long repressed may be so frightening that it leads to a form of spiritual paralysis. When the past is too painful it may perhaps be more prudent to remain unforgiving.

It is sometimes thought that negative hateful thoughts cannot co-exist with forgiveness and that love must now replace hate, but a mature forgiving needs to reconcile both elements, the love and the hate. It does not deny the evil that has occurred, but it also recognises the humanity of the offender.

This century has seen the most enormous cruelties from the concentration camps to the slaughtering of ethnic minorities. Is it asking the impossible for the perpetrators of such evil to be forgiven? Perhaps the aggressive feelings that such evil arouses are simply too powerful to be integrated into positive feelings, leaving the forgiving process impossible. It becomes impossible to recognise any good in the people who behaved so badly, and the splitting becomes even more marked in an inability to see that a whole nation could not be totally responsible for what was done in its name.

J. Gartner asks the question that, if there is a mature forgiveness, is there also an immature forgiving? There can be a rather superior air to the one who does the forgiving, often leaving the forgiven one with feelings of inferiority. This is an attitude that is not unfamiliar to people in religious circles, where non-believers can be seen as wicked and in need of conversion.

It is not difficult to see how people can be cast into an outer darkness and condemned as damned. A therapist would see this as an example of projecting out the disturbing feelings of the one who condemns, so allowing them to expel their own dark side into the one condemned whilst at the same time remaining superior. Nations can use the same process when they demonise their enemies as has been seen in recent wars in Vietnam and Iraq.

Anthony de Mello tells the following story:

> Two Buddhist monks, on their way to the monastery, found an exceedingly beautiful woman on the river bank. Like them she wished to cross the river, but the water was too high. So one of the monks lifted her on to his back and carried her across.
>
> His fellow monk was thoroughly scandalised. For full two hours he berated him on his negligence in keeping the Holy Rule: Had he forgotten that he was a monk? How dare he touch a woman? What would people say? And so on and so forth.
>
> The offending monk listened patiently to the never-ending sermon. Finally he broke in with, 'Brother, I dropped the woman at the river. Are you still carrying her'?

De Mello comments: 'When religious people endlessly chew on the sins of others, one suspects that the chewing affords more pleasure than the sinning affords the sinner'.

While there is undoubted satisfaction in the immediate venting of anger and revenge, the holding of these feelings is self-defeating in the long run, since it endows them with energy. Often the ones who have offended are closely connected to the victim — parents, sibling, spouse, or close friends. A desire to take revenge can fatally undermine any hope of harmony with the people one loves. It is sad to read of family members who have fallen out and not spoken for years, or to hear of neighbours who bankrupt each other over boundary disputes.

CONCLUSION

The Christian knows that forgiveness is at the heart of their faith. The whole process of confession, repentance and atonement is the Christian model for healing the splitting and projections which are at the root of separation from God and from each other. Jesus was crucified for claiming to forgive sins, a strong reminder that forgiveness is painful. It frequently means swallowing one's pride, admitting that criticism and rejection, neglect and ingratitude, both hurt and sting. Ironically the more harshly we condemn others the more attracted we may be to the behaviour we condemn, or the more punishing our own conscience may be. It is a paradox of forgiveness that in forgiving others one can begin to forgive oneself.

The Masai villager had no escape. Without forgiveness, life is dire.

BIBLIOGRAPHY

Coate, M. A. (1994) *Sin, Guilt and Forgiveness*, London: SPCK
Donovan, V. J. (1982) *Christianity Rediscovered,* London: SCM Press
Gartner, J. (1988) 'The Capacity to Forgive', *Journal of Religion and Health*, Vol. 27, No. 4
De Mello, A. (1983) *The Song of the Bird*, Anand: Anand-Press

QUESTIONS

1 Are there some acts that cannot be forgiven?

2 Is it possible to forgive the perpetrators of genocide or of child sexual abuse and torture, especially if you are the parents, son or daughter?

3 Is forgiveness about guilt or is it about shame?

4 How meaningful are the acts of repentance that precede communion services?

Towards a Deeper Communion: Spirituality at the turn of the Millennium

Leslie Morley

As a new century begins we move into it shaped by the experiences of the previous one. The last century of the 2nd millennium has been scourged by war and inhumanity on a vast scale. The slaughter of the First World War, the experience of the holocaust, together with the genocide and ethnic cleansing of more recent years, have undermined the confidence in human progress which marked the spirit of the age as this century began. Confidence in the capacity of human beings to solve the problems of famine, poverty and international debt has been weakened by a growing disparity between the rich and the poor nations. This has had its impact on how God is to be understood and how he is to be known.

Writing in the introduction to a new revision of *Forms of Prayer for Jewish Worship*, the prayer book of the Reformed Synagogues of Great Britain published in 1985, the editors express the hope that it will become a source book of Jewish spirituality as well as a book for public services. New material has therefore been added 'to join our present needs to the faith we have received'. It is significant for our understanding of spirituality today that much of this material does not come from the writings of clergy or theologians but from unexpected places. The editors note that:

> In the confusion of our times, the word of God has come to us (as perhaps it always has) in unexpected ways and through unexpected people; in social workers' reports, on wrapping paper found in a concentration camp, or written on cellar walls in time of persecution. We find our spirituality in the diaries of an adolescent girl, in the records of ghetto doctors, and in the honesty of modern Jewish writers. In diverse ways they experienced the great realities and their words are words of truth. They are His witnesses to us, willing or unwilling, conscious or unconscious of their burden.

Here is evidence that at the beginning of a new millennium we find our spirituality not in the manuals which attempted to chart and systematise spiritual progress but in the raw material of human experience. This is further reflected in the memorial erected last year to the 'Martyrs of the Twentieth Century'. Ten were chosen to represent perhaps hundreds more.

They are commemorated with statues on the west front of Westminster Abbey. They come from different parts of the world and their suffering reflects the horrors of this age, an age of dictators, of racial hatred, of suspicion and poverty, of mass murder and of tyranny. In their faithfulness to the way of love the light of hope was not extinguished. God comes to us now in the fragments of human lives and in the midst of our human poverty and brokenness. This may be the appropriate way in which God is apprehended in our age for there is a deep distrust of overarching systems of meaning. If truth comes to us in these fragments it may be that Jesus' command to his disciples after the feeding of the multitude to 'gather up the fragments that nothing be lost' takes on a new importance as, like the editors of the Jewish *Forms of Prayer*, we try to discern and hold together the authentic voices of those who encounter God in the uncertainties of human existence.

Of course there is a danger of sliding either into a form of fundamentalism or into a spirituality that is in the end more self-regarding than self-transcending. As the Dominican Simon Tugwell has observed:

> We clutch at our bits of truth and force them into a pattern, when the key to the whole puzzle is still missing. We make sense of our religion, of our world in the twilight of our own ingenuity, without daring to wait for the full daylight of God's final disclosure of himself and his works. And then, God forgive us, we do battle for our truths, not because they are true but because they are ours.

Tugwell argues that we must live with the provisional in our understanding of God. And surely it has always been so for the ultimate unknowability of God means we can never grasp fully all that God is nor can we claim to have discerned all his paths. This is disconcerting, for human beings prefer certainties but the Christian religion rejoices in the mystery of God and the call to holiness means living by faith and not by certainty. The call of God does not mean finding security in the absolutes of an ideology nor in the exclusivity of a particular identity group or sect but in the mystery of his presence and his unfolding work of saving love. In the next century the Church faces the challenge of helping Christians to live with the provisional. The provisional rather than the absolute needs to be the mark of Christian faith and spirituality in the face of what seems to be the growing force of fundamentalism, in either its religious guise or its secular expression in certain forms of nationalism and racism.

The other danger, as I have indicated, is the temptation to select only those fragments of truth that suit me and with which I feel comfortable. The present burgeoning interest in spiritualities of every kind appears at times to be just another expression of the contemporary concern with self.

Spirituality is in danger of being a commodity that people choose for themselves, to suit their emotional preferences and to enhance their quality of life. But spirituality is lived faith not an add on to a chosen lifestyle option. As such it cannot be detached from the content of faith nor the challenges of the gospel. In this it presents a challenge to much of the individualism and privatisation in contemporary culture which so diminishes our understanding of what it means to be human.

Here I think we meet another aspect of the spiritual agenda at the turn of the millennium — how to be human? Human self-understanding in the West has been forged on an identification of the human person with the individual. This has brought many freedoms and an appropriate concern for individual rights. Yet it also implies that in some fundamental way we each stand over against the other and that any coming together is based on mutual self-interest. There is, however, another way of understanding what it is to be human that is more in keeping with the Christian vision and with the story of our own emotional and psychological development from the womb to adulthood. 'A person is a person through other persons' is a Xhosa saying, but it expresses very clearly the truth that our identity is a gift and that a person cannot be a person in isolation but only in unity with others. To identify with oneself as an individual is a sign of human fallenness not of our created nature. After all, I do not exist in myself but only because God has spoken my name and called me into being, and it is the nature of the Love that loved me into his likeness that I should come to understand that 'my neighbour is myself'. To be truly human is to be in communion with others. Individual human rights alone cannot satisfy the longings of creatures made in the image of the Persons of the Trinity.

Now this has implications among other things for prayer. The opening of the heart and mind to God in prayer involves a deepening compassion and leads the person who prays into a profound solidarity with their fellow human beings in all circumstances. Prayer deepens communion and does not reinforce divisions. The prayer group whose members begin to regard themselves as rather superior sorts of Christians have lost their way in prayer. Prayer sensitises and unites. So I am hesitant about the well meant expression, 'There but for the grace of God go I'. I am sure that in circumstances in which we might want to use it we should be saying, 'There by the grace of God am I', for the grace of God enables me to see my sister or brother as one with myself. Their sorrow is my sorrow, their joy is my joy. It was the wisdom of the Desert Fathers that led them to say, 'I am my neighbour'. St Isaac of Syria, a 7th-century bishop and hermit, in a passage in his writings which seems to come out of the past and accosts us with an astonishing contemporaneity, extends this embrace of compassion to all creation:

> What is a compassionate heart? It is a heart on fire for the whole of creation, for humanity, for the birds, for the animals, for demons and all that exists. At the recollection and at the sight of them such a person's eyes overflow with tears owing to the vehemence of the compassion which grips his heart; as a result of his deep mercy his heart shrinks and cannot bear to look on any injury or the slightest suffering of anything in creation. This is why he constantly offers up prayer full of tears, even for the irrational animals and for the enemies of truth, even for those who harm him, so that they may be protected and find mercy.

Isaac is a man gripped by the love of God. That is what shapes and controls his spirituality. Encounter with the love of God has given birth in him to new depths of compassion, a sharing of God's love for all creation and a longing for the reconciliation of all creation. For Isaac the love of God is not divided and so his own compassion must extend to the demons and the enemies of truth and he must pray for them and for their salvation. In the following passage with its marvellous image of creation restored he sees the recovery of the human vocation in the light of Christ's coming and as crucial to the reconciliation of all creation:

> The humble man approaches wild animals, and the moment they catch sight of him their ferocity is tamed. They come up and cling to him as to their Master, wagging their tails and licking his hands and feet. They sense as coming from him the same fragrance that came from Adam before the transgression, the time when they were gathered together before him and he gave them their names in Paradise. This scent has been taken away from us, but Christ has renewed it and given it back to us at his coming. It is this which has sweetened the fragrance of humanity. Even the demons in their malice and fierceness, and with all the pride of their minds, become like dust once they have encountered a humble person.

St Isaac offers us a strangely contemporary vision of what it means to be human and a spirituality that lacks all feeling of triumphalism. God is for him a humble God. 'Humility', he writes, 'is the robe of the Godhead.' The power of God is his all-embracing love. He does not compel, for violence is foreign to him. He does not seek to dominate humanity because he himself is not subject to domination by any force and has no need therefore to dominate in order to avoid being dominated himself.

A spirituality such as St Isaac offers us must also issue in changes in disposition, in outlook and in action. It cannot become a spirituality of self-regard but by its nature must involve engagement with the world and shape the way of being human in the world. It does not emphasise competition with other faiths or spiritualities but dialogue. In the next century the Church will face the challenge of helping its members to engage with the world and to see it as the focus of God's love. There will be a temptation for the Church to turn inward in reaction to the world's benign neglect of it and so to become overly concerned about the size of its membership rather than with discovering and celebrating that way of being human which embraces all creation and which Christ's coming makes possible. T. S. Eliot wrote in *The Four Quartets*:

> Old men ought to be explorers
> Here or there does not matter
> We must be still and still moving
> Into another intensity
> For a further union, a deeper communion.

The arrival of a new millennium provides us with an opportunity to renew our hope, to be in dialogue with the saints of the past who still speak to us and who offer us a large vision of God's love and purposes, and to go on being explorers. It is not just 'old men' who ought to be explorers in faith but young and old alike, women and men, seeking that other intensity, that further union and deeper communion that is the Kingdom of God.

QUESTIONS

1 Bearing in mind the comments of the editors of the Jewish *Forms of Prayer* where have you discovered fragments of God in unexpected places?

2 Should we as Christians be world affirming or world denying?

Issues of Sexuality

Jeni Parsons

SEXUALITY, our embodiedness — our 'being bodies', does not go away, nor could it. The affirmation of the Hebrew Bible in Genesis that creation was 'very good' has never allowed Christianity to disappear completely down the path labelled 'Body bad: Spirit good' though theologians all through our history have tried! That dualism of body and mind, or flesh and spirit, can never satisfactorily account for who we are or who God is. We can't see ourselves as minds/spirits trapped inside a body and remain true to the Incarnation where we believe that 'the Word became flesh and dwelt among us' and is still becoming flesh. To think dualistically and to make God only spirit removes God from passion and removes God from humanity. To remove God from passion means removing God from loving and suffering and delighting, and removes humanity from the embrace of the One known in Jesus of Nazareth and in the loving, suffering and delighting of other people. We need our bodies to worship God, to know one another and to be known.

In thinking about sexuality Christians have often begun by asking first what the Bible and Tradition have to say about it and have then chosen certain passages to reinforce particular views, common in their society at the time, about sexual relations, marriage, celibacy and related matters. These they have then applied to their own lives, or more often, to the lives of others. Instead, I want us to think first about sexuality and our own experience before we come to Scripture and Tradition, so that we can try to take account of what it is to be 'embodied' in the new millennium as Christians rather than decide what sexuality is 'allowed/disallowed' and then apply it to ourselves and others. In this way the diversity of our experience will be apparent and does not immediately, if at all, have to be ranked as 'best/most Christian' or anything else. It is in our human experience of ourselves, other people and the world around us that we discover new ways of looking at God and being looked at by God, of challenging traditions and being challenged by them, and how to live out the gospel daily.

In Europe and North America our lives are often very much longer than they would have been if we had been born in the Middle East 2,000 years ago. We also understand much more about our own biology and psychology than was known at the time of Jesus' birth. Perhaps the biggest difference between early Christians and us in Europe and North America, in terms of culture, is the relative position of women. Reliable contraception, economic independence, education and employment all serve to allow women a greater opportunity to make choices about their lives and sexual expression. Heterosexual sexual activity does not carry with it the risk of pregnancy for women which it did in the past. Gay and lesbian sexuality is now comprehended as a part of the variety of human sexual experience. Slavery in Europe and North America has formally been abolished, including sexual slavery, and the law mostly attempts to protect the rights of individuals and groups to conduct their sexual lives in the way that suits them. That this is the cultural and social context in which we are exploring sexuality has not taken account of our ethnic diversity, the economic variations of class, nor the fast-changing nature of our cultures where my experience as a growing woman is not the same as my daughter's experience, nor is it the same as my mother's. All these features are important in talking about sexuality, as indeed they are in any discussion, because there has been the assumption, still widely held, that it is possible to talk as though none of these factors affected our conversation. In effect what was considered the norm was the male experience, the white experience, the middle-class and the heterosexual experience. Now this is being challenged on several fronts and so our discussion of sexuality should take into account who is talking.

Sexuality isn't easy to define. It is more than what genital sexual acts people engage in, though it includes that too. Sexuality is a necessary part of having a body through which we know others and are known by them. It is about more than whether we are female or male biologically, though it is also about that. It is more than having reached the age of consent since sexuality doesn't belong only to the adult but is also part of the life of the child. Sexuality is expressed by the person who chooses celibacy as much as it is by the person who over their lifetime has many sexual partners. Sexuality is about relationships including friendship. Yet sexuality remains hard to pin down. In the same way one might say that spirituality is equally hard to define, and this is no accident. Sexuality and spirituality are both about relationship, both about bodies, both about souls and both about what it means to be a person in community with others. Both are concerned with integrity, with the match between values and actions, and both at their best, many would argue, have self-giving love as their hallmark of authenticity. In both, the holy mystery of how in losing my life I find it, is encountered. Spirituality is as much to do with how I vote as with how I pray and sexuality as much to do with how I pray as it is with my delight in my lover.

So, think for a minute about how you are experienced by other people you know: you are a body — usually clothed — with hair, eyes, skin of a particular colour and texture, with expression and animation, conversation and attention. In relating to you those who encounter you encounter your body at a distance or more closely. They form opinions to be affirmed or corrected later about whether you are open to their presence or not. They also, on coming closer, encounter the more intimate you, imparted by tone in speaking, facial and other movement, smell and demeanour. Who we are is at the very least mediated to others through our bodies, and without them, as in the Internet chat rooms where bodies are not visible and even the sex of a person is often undeclared, we would probably say we could not be properly known. Perhaps it is in that old-fashioned biblical word 'to know' which was used for sexual knowing that we can find some ways forward in our quest to grapple with the issue of sexuality for the next millennium.

St Paul's hope that we will 'know as we are known' by God implies an intimacy that Paul could only long for but not yet fully accomplish. At the time he saw God only 'in a glass darkly' but 'then face to face'. Paul's desire to behold God, to know God, is the quest of the mystics whose experience has been spiritual certainly but also very often sexual. That is, their desire for God has inflamed their whole person so that their mind/heart longs for God and so does their flesh/body. To read the 16th-century nun Teresa of Avila or the 14th-century Julian of Norwich, Bernard of Clairvaux in the 12th century or many of the other mystics, is to hear that crackle of electricity that lovers know with their beloved. Such whole-hearted knowing or longing-to-know is the stuff of mysticism and the stuff of sexuality. Do you remember the longing to know someone better, the desire for the beloved, the deep commitment of a passionate friendship, the sheer delight in the naked embrace of your lover? Do you know that moment of first holding your own child and the accompanying fierceness and protectiveness, the pleasure of touch when a friend hugs you, the feeling of sun on your face or the wind at your back? It is through our alert bodies that we know God and other people, and through our enlivened bodies that we are known both by God and by other people.

We are capable of hiding who we are from God, from other people and even from ourselves, and we are capable of disclosing ourselves too. In spirituality and in sexuality the quality and depth of a relationship depends on the level of disclosure and on the willingness to give up distortions of who we are in the belief that we are made in the image of God as Genesis declares. The challenge for the churches in the millennium with regard to sexuality and thereby to spirituality too is to be open to the exploration of what God is like in those who are unlike us. Over the last two millennia the church has asked women to hide their sexuality for fear of discovering too much more of the image of God even though 'in the image of God He created him, male and female he created them'. Now the church still desires that gay men and lesbians hide their sexuality for fear that God may also be found in the love which such men and women know to be true.

If we turn to the gospels in our desire for God in the next millennium we find a Jesus who spoke mostly about money rather than sex, who never criticised those who followed in the crowd, the embodied poor and diseased, the ones excluded from status, acceptability and the world of worship. It is the sins of hardness of heart, contempt for the poor, and the idolatry of things that Jesus condemns. A spirituality that commits us to the struggle for justice, to openness to God wherever God is to be found, and to the living of lives shaped by respect, passion and the search for equality also equips us to explore a sexuality that is concerned for intimacy, delight and equality. The desire of one group to try to claim all the truth and rightness as belonging to them alone cannot stand up against the variety of human experience and of faithful Christian living which knows God through the intimacy, delight and vulnerable equality of friendships and sexual relationships. By starting with our experience, and that of others, of sexuality and spirituality and their connectedness, we are no longer able to compress them back into the box of 'thou shalt not' so beloved of some parts of the church and society. The abundant life promised by Jesus as God's gift to the world is springing up in places we had not previously allowed to exist. Of course such places have always existed but have been hidden through fear and by repression. The opportunity to relook at sexuality in the new millennium is aided by a growing openness to feminist thought and gay and lesbian people's experience that says to the churches, '"God's love has been shed abroad in our hearts by the Holy Spirit he has given to us" — how is it with you?' I believe that in the new millennium we need to give up trying to live Christian lives as if we had no bodies and recommit ourselves to the God who became flesh so that we might learn how to live and to love.

QUESTIONS

1 In what ways has your experience of sexuality differed from that of your parents?

2 To what extent do you use your body in worship?

3 What is the connection between a passion for justice, a passion for God and your own sexuality?

4 How would you like the church to be changed by God's passion for the world?

Multi-Faith Society

Helen Reid

THIS year we celebrate the year AD 2000, two millennia since the birth of our Saviour, Jesus Christ. For Muslims, however, it is the year 1420 because the Islamic calendar begins with the *Hijra*, when the Prophet Muhammad migrated from Makkah to Medina. For Jews it is 5760 because the Jewish calendar begins from the traditional date of creation, while in 1999, Sikhs celebrated 300 years since the formation of the community of baptised Sikhs (the *Khalsa*).

There is clearly a diversity of dates and celebrations among the British people and this reflects the diversity found throughout the world. As Christians we are aware of religious diversity and seek to relate this to our commitment to our Christian faith. We need to find ways to maintain our own faith integrity and also to live peacefully with all our neighbours.

This discussion paper explores some of the issues associated with life in a multi-faith society for Christians in the 3rd millennium. It focuses on Britain, rather than the world context, and the relevance of inter-faith issues to our daily lives. It aims to encourage Christians to reflect on the multi-faith nature of Britain at the start of the new millennium and to prepare for genuine sharing with people of other faiths in the years ahead. It is time to face the challenging questions that our multi-faith society raises for us and to take up the exciting opportunities that it offers.

FAITH GROUPS IN BRITAIN

People belong to and identify with different religious faiths in Britain including: Ba'hai, Brahma Kumari, Buddhism, Christianity, Hinduism, Jainism, Judaism, Islam, Rastafarianism, Sikhism and Taoism. Some of these faith groups contain different denominations or sects. Other people have no religious faith and may be agnostic, atheist, humanist or secular.

In Britain there are often links between particular faith groups and ethnic backgrounds. These can be summarised as follows:

- Christianity: the majority of Christians in Britain have White British ethnicity. Some have African, African-Caribbean, Asian, Chinese, South American ethnicities or other European ethnicities, such as Greek, Irish and Polish
- Hinduism: the majority of Hindus have Indian ethnicity
- Islam: over half of British Muslims have South Asian ethnicity, mostly

Bangladeshi and Pakistani. There are also African, African-Caribbean, Middle Eastern, South-East Asian and White British Muslims
- Judaism: the majority of Jews in Britain have family origins in Central and Eastern Europe or the former Soviet Union
- Sikhism: the majority of Sikhs have Indian Punjabi ethnicity.

These links between faith and ethnicity indicate that inter-faith relationships may also be inter-ethnic group relationships. As a result, relationships between people of different faiths are not just about different religious beliefs, they may also encompass different ethnic or cultural backgrounds. The section in this book on racism, therefore, has insights to offer our reflection on inter-faith issues.

CHRISTIANS IN A MULTI-FAITH SOCIETY

It has been shown that the population of Britain includes people of different faiths, cultures and ethnic backgrounds. This means that for many people inter-faith relationships are a part of everyday life in their neighbourhoods, workplaces and, for some, in their families. Many other people do not live in multi-faith areas of the country. They do still experience the multi-faith nature of British society, however, through home mission as part of a national church, newspapers and television, and Religious Education lessons in schools. There is, therefore, a need for all Christians in Britain to reflect on what it means to live in a multi-faith society.

Such reflection on today's multi-faith society needs to include a search for ways to act in accordance with Christian teaching. When we look to the New Testament for guidance, however, we do not find a well-developed or detailed approach to living alongside people of other faiths. This is because it was written in a particular time and place, and Jesus did not encounter Hindus or Buddhists during his ministry, for example, as we do in our lives today. Consequently, New Testament passages require some interpretation before we can apply their teachings to our everyday lives in a multi-faith society.

In the limited space of this paper I would like to reflect on one aspect of Jesus' ministry that may illuminate the arena of inter-faith relationships. During his ministry Jesus spoke with and shared with a wide variety of people. He often spent time with people who lived on the margins of society, such as tax collectors and prostitutes (see Matthew 9:9–13, Mark 2:13–17 and Luke 5:27–32). He also spoke with people outside the main group such as the Syro-Phoenician woman (Matthew 15:21–28 and Mark 7:24–30). Such an open and inclusive approach was criticised by many people and at times it may have surprised even his own disciples. For example, in Mark 9:38–40 and Luke 9:49–50 we read that the disciples came to Jesus and spoke of a man who claimed to cast out demons in his name. Jesus' response was not that this man should be stopped because, he said, 'Whoever is not against us is for us'.

When challenged by claims that a man outside his group was casting out demons in his name, Jesus did not respond in an exclusive, defensive way. Rather he responded openly and with confidence. This encourages us to respond to people of other faiths in an open and confident way. We must be brave enough to share with our neighbours of other faiths in the challenges of contemporary life and adopt an open approach to living in a multi-faith society.

How to live according to an open and inclusive approach needs to be considered in the light of the teaching that as Christians we are called to mission. Does this teaching mean that inter-faith relationships are an opportunity for evangelism? We must weigh up carefully the different and complementary elements of Christian mission: loving service and proclamation of the Gospel. When we reach out to people of other faiths we must find ways of service, take time to learn about what is important to them (including their faith) and get to know them as people. Through such love and service we may earn the right to speak of our faith. This does not necessarily mean that people of other faiths will become Christians and join churches, but they will witness the love of Jesus in our lives. In our attempts to forge inter-faith relationships we must approach others with openness and love, honesty and respect, at all times and in all circumstances.

WHAT DOES IT ACTUALLY MEAN TO BE INVOLVED IN INTER-FAITH ACTIVITIES?

The multi-faith nature of Britain is an important part of both our spiritual and social life. In terms of the spiritual dimension there are opportunities for sharing and learning together with people of other faiths through dialogue. Moreover, at a time when as a society we face many social and economic challenges, people of different faiths can work together in social action initiatives. Such inter-faith co-operation leads to positive relationships between people of different faiths and a working towards making our society a better place for all to live.

INTER-FAITH DIALOGUE

Dr Elizabeth Harris, Inter-Faith Officer for the Methodist Church, has been involved in inter-faith dialogue for many years. She speaks of the excitement and joy of creating friendship across faiths and acknowledges the potential this offers for growth in one's own faith. In particular, some of the Buddhist-Christian dialogue in which she has taken part has opened up new areas of development for her Christian life. For example, there are Buddhist feminists who are rediscovering the inspiring stories of nuns who have been overlooked in the recent telling of Buddhist history. Christian women can gain confidence from this and look for role models within Christian history to inspire and encourage them. In this way a sharing of the insights of another faith can lead to a greater appreciation of one's own Christian faith.

JOINT SOCIAL ACTION

Christians who live in multi-faith areas often feel particularly called to reach out to their neighbours of other faiths. In many instances this is not to speak directly about their faith, as in inter-faith dialogue, but to share in everyday concerns about family and community life. People of different faiths have much in common as fellow human beings and local neighbours. For example, a church in an area of Bradford called Frizinghall is surrounded by Muslim and secular neighbours. People at this church felt called to involve themselves further in community life with these neighbours. Following a day of prayer in June 1996 they established a Parent and Toddler Group called PATCH (this stands for Play At The Church). This group provides a safe and stimulating environment for babies and toddlers to play and develop social skills. It runs two sessions a week which are attended by 87 adults and children. Roughly half of those who attend are Asian Muslim parents and children. Their involvement has come about through personal invitations to individuals, for example neighbours, and recommendations by health visitors. They are also encouraged by the involvement of three Asian nursery nurses on college placements with PATCH.

Church members support the work of PATCH with prayer, practical help and volunteering to run the sessions. They believe it is important that both Christians and people of other faiths are involved in this project because this reflects the make-up of the local community. PATCH is just one example of inter-faith social action and there are many other ways that people of different faiths can work together. Often these opportunities arise in local multi-faith areas but there are also opportunities nationally, for example, through NCH Action for Children and internationally, for example, through Christian Aid.

PRAYING FOR OUR MULTI-FAITH SOCIETY

As Christians we bring our concerns before God in prayer and assert the importance of prayer in our lives, thoughts and actions. This importance holds true for our concern with inter-faith issues. We need, therefore, to build a prayerful integrity into our involvement in our multi-faith society and our engagement in inter-faith dialogue and action. This can include praying for people and communities of other faiths and for the building of peaceful inter-faith relationships.

Many Christians may find it a challenge to pray for those of another faith, even to know how to begin to do so. Yet in the multi-faith city of Bradford, for example, many Christians pray for people of other faiths. They pray as part of a commitment to their city and the people who live there. The following prayer was written from this commitment and experience at the Touchstone Methodist Centre in Bradford. Christians, including those who do not live in multi-faith areas of the country, may feel able to share in it.

> Lord, we offer you our multi-faith society;
> we bring before you for blessing
> creative and energising opportunities...
>
> for developing friendships across faiths
> for celebrating diversity in community life
> for acting jointly for a brighter future
>
> ...and we give you thanks
>
> Lord, we offer you our multi-faith society;
> we bring before you for blessing
> the pain of people lost...
>
> those who are discouraged from practising their faith
> those who are abused for the colour of their skin
> those who are perplexed by the changes in society
>
> ...and we seek your grace
>
> Lord, we offer you our multi-faith society;
> we commend to you its faith communities
> and bring before you for blessing
> our struggles for justice and peace.
>
> Amen.

The opportunities for inter-faith activities and reflection outlined in this paper show that in recent decades many Christians have come to recognise the challenges and opportunities of living in a multi-faith society. They have sought to learn about other faiths and to establish peaceful relationships and co-operative partnerships with people of other faiths. Such responses recognise the vitality of faith groups in our society and the richness that is to be found in the diversity of faiths. Together, people of different faiths can work towards better mutual understanding and make Britain and the world a better place for all to live.

BIBLIOGRAPHY

Wesley Ariarajah (1995) *The Bible and People of other Faiths*, Geneva: World Council of Churches

QUESTIONS

1 Identity has many aspects. Make a list or tell a friend about the many aspects of your identity, for example, Christian, mother, Welsh. How might an appreciation of the different aspects of your identity support your reflection on inter-faith relationships?

2 In what ways are inter-faith issues and activities relevant to your local situation?

3 Are inter-faith activities mutually worthwhile?

Consider the two following questions:

4 What have Christians to offer others in inter-faith engagement?

5 What might Christians gain through inter-faith engagement?

What Future for Religious Education?

Cathy Michell

RELIGIOUS EDUCATION in schools has always had the power simultaneously to arouse public controversy and public apathy on a grand scale. Any writer on the subject therefore takes their courage into both hands and steps forward not quite knowing whether a minefield or a sleepy pasture awaits their wary tread. It is obvious, however, that any exploration of RE's possible future needs to tangle with a number of key issues. The intention of this essay is to look at these in turn. They are:

- The context in which the teaching of RE in schools takes place; the nature of modern British culture, especially with regard to the role and status of religion in our society.
- The unique history and character of RE itself which marks it out as a peculiarly British, or rather English phenomenon, quite different from possible equivalents in the rest of Europe and certainly in complete contradiction to the American solution.
- Questions arising from an examination of both RE's social context and its special character which may point to its future; specifically about the subject's aims and ideals, content, status (including mundane but crucial realities such as money, time, staff training etc.) and relationships with various public bodies and communities ranging from government to pupils and parents.

It is now accepted without debate, certainly in the world of modern RE, that Britain is a multi-cultural and multi-faith place. This is particularly obvious in urban centres such as Wembley or Southall, Birmingham, Leicester or Bradford. Here the minarets, domes and flags of the world's great religions punctuate the city landscape, witness to the hard work, emerging identity and devoted commitment of the migrant communities whose sacred buildings they grace. But even in smaller towns and rural places bereft of such noticeable cultural or religious richness, the presence of individuals or families, of Indian, Bangladeshi, Chinese, Pakistani or Turkish businesses, the glimpse of a colourful sari, an overheard shred of Italian or Polish, brings home what the media also confirms, that we are indeed an increasingly diverse, plural society.

Whilst it is relatively straightforward to recognise, 'label' (and roughly to number) minority religious communities such as Sikhs, Muslims or Hindus, it is far more difficult to define the religious character of the majority. British society has been described both as 'secular' and 'post-Christian' but these terms are misleading for a number of reasons.

By the mid-1990s there remained something like 6.5 million formal members of the various Christian denominations. According to the University of Derby's exhaustive 'multi faith directory', *Religions in the UK*, some 38 million people regard themselves as in some way, however vestigially, Christian. Certainly until quite recently Britain could have been regarded — and still is by some — as a Christian society, if 'Christian' is defined as broadly as the directory advises. It is obvious from these estimates that rather than a nation of church-goers allied to traditional Christian orthodoxy we have increasingly moved into a kind of 'diffusive Christianity'. Tinged with a vaguely Protestant ethos this 'Christianity' has been described by one writer as, 'long on practical ethics and occasional worship, short on theology and regular devotion' (Parsons 1995). It finds expression in the private sphere by an occasional dipping into the churches for specific individual or family needs, for example, key rites of passage — 'hatch, match and despatch' — for which there are no satisfying alternatives elsewhere, and the celebration of particular festivals. It emerges in such things as the valuing of the ten commandments as a blueprint for knowing 'the difference between right and wrong'; respect for the moral teaching and example of Jesus the man; sending children to Sunday school or church-affiliated uniformed youth organisations; switching on 'Thought for the Day' or watching 'Songs of Praise'. In the public domain it is there on Remembrance Sunday and at times of national crisis or mourning and it is mixed up somehow in the interface between monarchy, Government and Established Church.

Until quite recently, perhaps up until the early 1970s, this 'basic', 'essential', popular Christianity was sustained by institutions such as the Sunday School movement and the BBC which saw its overall ethos and mission in Christian terms and its religious broadcasting as entirely and explicitly so. In the nation's schools religious education and worship functioned with the same agenda. Since then, however, whilst still not entirely 'post-Christian', the British have continued to draw away even from the diffused faith outlined above. This on-going process of dilution has had as its backdrop the continuing decline in rates of committed membership to and involvement in the traditional denominations, a downwards trend largely unaffected by the 'success' of the charismatic, community, black and other conservative evangelical churches. It has been expressed in the significant shifts in emphasis which have occurred in the two indicators already mentioned, that is in the fields of broadcasting and education. Both of these have largely abandoned their explicitly Christian character and Christianising aims. As the Report on the Future of Broadcasting spelt out in 1977, religion in Britain was 'no longer synonymous with Christianity'. Therefore religious programmes should not reflect solely the life of the mainstream churches but rather 'present a *religious* interpretation of the world rather than a specifically Christian interpretation' (my italics). Broadcasting had now to acknowledge a great plurality of world views to embrace and satisfy the needs of the majority outside the churches, those without any specific allegiance, as well as people from the other religious traditions represented in British society.

In 1867 the poet Matthew Arnold, standing 'On Dover Beach', heard only the 'melancholy, long, withdrawing roar' of the retreating 'sea of faith'. It is apparent that in some ways his observation about his own society (post the 1851 religious census which so shook the churches then) is being borne out in our own. Thus whilst remaining a 'Christian' culture in numerical terms — the Church still being the largest religious institution in the country — and in terms of the nation's history and its Christian cultural legacy in art, music, literature and custom, Christianity in Britain is steadily leaching away. A *post-Christian* society we may well become but Arnold's pessimism and modern visions of a secular present or future do not fit what is emerging religiously here. Instead it is now obvious that numerous *alternative* beliefs and spiritualities are springing up in the fertile ground of the very late 20th century. Some, like the various Buddhist traditions or the Hare Krishnas (ISKCON), have been adopted and adapted from the world's great faith traditions. Some have been created this century by individuals such as Rudolf Steiner (Anthroposophical Society), L. Ron Hubbard (Church of Scientology), or Sun Myung Moon (The Moonies). These are often referred to as 'New Religious Movements' and it is estimated that there are about 500 of them active in the country (HMSO 1992). Others have roots in the sub-soil of mysticism or folklore where Celt, Viking and Pagan twine together, or borrow freely from religions ancient and modern to combine an individual pot-pourri of faith and practice made all the more fragrant with sprinklings of yoga, aromatherapy, Feng Shui, incense, candles, crystals, star readings, reflexology or herbalism. Mixed and shaken, this post-modern cocktail has been labelled 'New Age'. It is characterised by concern for the environment and for the whole planet understood as a living organism. It rejects the conventional Western rationalist, scientific world-view and looks back to ideal, pre-urban, pre-scientific cultures, and it has a preoccupation with the nature and development of the self, often expressed by interest in the healing of body, mind and spirit. Widespread belief in reincarnation is a natural adjunct of this focus on self, offering a more satisfying account for many of the meaning of their individual life in a century of rapid change and uncertainty.

There is no need to stand on Arnold's dreary beach nor even to go on muddy pilgrimage to Glastonbury to appreciate the 'veritable universe of faiths mingling in cheerful and eclectic confusion' (Parsons 1995) which characterises the modern religious scene in Britain. As Steve Bruce (1995) discovered and any of us may easily confirm, the shelves of local bookshops are packed with the New Age (Bruce found 70 metres to 5 metres of shelf space for Christianity, in the Aberdeen branch of Waterstones!). Here is the 'pick 'n' mix', the self-service cafeteria counter, the supermarket, shopping mall, DIY choice of infinite colour, fluidity and variety which constitutes the far from secular reality of 'religion' in our society. This is the context in which RE in schools finds itself today.

All sorts of misapprehensions, coupled with a whole range of conflicting attitudes towards it, serve to obscure the real nature and position of RE in 'maintained' or state-sector schools. It remains entangled, in the minds of the public (and media, churches and politicians too), with 'assemblies' — school worship — and events such as school nativity plays. Parallel to this is the belief that the subject's chief aim is to teach children to be religious in some way, ideally Christian, but in any case to have a perceivable effect on their moral standards and future ability to choose a faith for themselves. Mixed up with this hope is one which envisages better citizens and the reinforcement of national identity. In order to deliver this, RE teachers are thought to have a special vocation. Believers themselves, their special role is to act as moral and religious exemplars facilitating their pupils' development in these crucial areas of human growth and enculturation. The churches, and particularly the Established church, are felt to have natural expertise in the field and are therefore thought to be legitimately involved in the oversight and delivery of the subject. Ideally RE should not be regarded as a 'subject' at all but rather a moral and spiritual ethos pervading and underpinning every aspect of the school community's life, finding expression in disciplined, purposeful action and harmonious, respectful relationships. If not a subject then RE is not 'academic', cannot and ought not to be examined in any way and is consequently to be thought of as second rate in terms of, e.g. entrance to higher education. Rather oddly, the fact of its obligatory presence in the curriculum, coupled with dark suspicions that it is to do with 'indoctrination', gives force to this conviction about its intrinsic inferiority, whilst its absence from the National Curriculum and obvious 'Cinderella' status in terms of time-tabling, funding and teacher training, serve further to convince that it is all just too vague, irrelevant and undemanding!

So attitudes to RE present an unfortunate paradox. On the one hand, if it makes children, school and even national life 'better', more spiritual, more civilised, then it is to be highly valued and much sentiment may be lavished upon it. If it makes them Christian it won't do any harm and it might do some good as it forges common values to counter the mish-mash of faiths and 'races' which threaten to swamp British traditions and identity. However, on the other hand, if it pushes beliefs which the majority find unbelievable, whilst also only being of use when somehow vaguely diffused into community life, then it is damned either because it teaches nonsense or because it can no longer be distinguished from 'general' or 'personal and social' or citizenship or cultural education. Subsumed in these it conveniently disappears altogether.

It is not surprising that this range of misunderstandings and associated attitudes should adhere to RE. Its unique nature and peculiar position in England and Wales (it is different again in Scotland and Ireland) are the product of a long and complex history fraught with and productive of the confusions and prejudices noted above.

Religious teaching in schools was shaped from the 1830s onwards by processes which were eventually to result in the gradual emergence of a national education system. The early days of this process were characterised by power struggles between the churches themselves (Anglican and Nonconformist) and those churches and the state over provision and control of education. The religious education which grew from this tug-of-war between Church, Chapel and State was one hedged about by political compromise. In schools not under the control of the churches it was to be non-denominational. This was generally interpreted as sticking to simple exposition of the Bible ('Scripture'), certainly with no teaching of doctrine or creeds! There were to be 'conscience clauses' allowing withdrawal of children from teaching not conducive to their parents and no religious 'tests' or criteria for appointing teachers. To facilitate the accelerating absorption of Church schools into the maintained sector after 1918, so-called 'agreed syllabuses' drawn up by committees representative of the 'dual system' became the means by which the subject's aims and content were defined. This framework for 'Religious Instruction' as it was then called, was confirmed legally by the 1944 Education Act which further stipulated that both RI and school worship should from then on be mandatory.

By the 1920s when at last the 'religious difficulty' of the previous century had burnt itself out, RI settled into a mould within which it was to remain until the early 1970s. For half a century it was assumed that it must be essentially, unquestioningly Christian but bearing the stamp of no particular church. As the increasingly detailed introductions to contemporary agreed syllabuses reveal, those in charge of the subject, academics, teachers, churchmen and local government officials, concurred that RI must have a pivotal role in education and schools. For them it was not merely a discrete subject among others, its content must necessarily spill out to provide the underpinning for the whole curriculum and to influence all of the school's life. They spoke in grandiose and idealistic terms of RI's mission, hand in hand with school worship, to convert pupils. The 1949 Cambridgeshire syllabus proclaimed, for example, that,

> To teach Christianity to our children is to inspire them with the vision of the glory of God in the face of Jesus Christ, and to send them into the world willing to follow Him who was among us as one who serveth.

The aim of this 'Christian Education' was to make the school itself a Christian community, an 'ecclesia'. Ultimately, however, it was to recover and remake a Christian society in Britain. There was a yearning for a former golden era in the nation's history — medieval or Victorian — when culture bore the stamp of one dominant ideology, a Christianity purified of denominational accretion. Thus RI teachers (frequently likened to Jesus himself), rather than the churches, were to take responsibility for the re-Christianising of Britain and act to build their schools into bastions against the threatening individualism, scientism, secularism and materialism of the modern world.

This very pre-modernist vision of RI's power and glory was badly flawed, of course, having at least two major drawbacks. It contrasted oddly with the actual neglect of the subject at 'the chalk face', so to speak, and its dismally low status (people educated in this period have numerous horror stories to relate!). Furthermore, the inflated hopes attached to it simply failed to materialise. Whilst it might be argued that this RI contributed somehow to the continuing undercurrent of 'diffusive Christianity' in society discussed previously, on the whole children, schools and country remained impervious to conversion. Schools were perhaps too much the mirrors of their society rather than its pattern.

By the mid-60s even RI specialists themselves were depressed; as Ronald Goldman noted sadly, the subject had become 'rather like a protracted visit to a museum, ossified in a holy time and place, irrelevant to modern life' (1965). Change was needed and, as in many other aspects of society, this decade proved to be a catalyst-time, a moment of opportunity when modern life at last began to shrug off — as Dennis Potter's television dramas graphically portray — the certainties of the past. The 'Christian Education' mould, which had given form to the appropriately entitled 'Religious *Instruction*', began to break and what was soon more liberally to be called 'Religious *Education*' emerged as something very different.

The sea-change which occurred in thinking about RE found legal expression in the 1988 Education Act, a fact amazing to those who remember the extraordinary furore which the passage of the RE clauses of this act kicked up! People in the field during this period were unable to decide whether the acres of newsprint, the journal articles, hot debate in both Houses and a national fit of moral and spiritual angst stirred by the rhetoric of bishops, politicians such as John Patton and the forthright Baroness Cox, constituted good news or bad for their subject. For a glorious moment RE found itself once more, as of old, at the centre of nationwide controversy. Concerted attempts, however, to reinforce and restate its Christian content and mission did not meet with success. When the dust settled, and to a general sigh of relief from the professionals responsible for academic research, training teachers and teaching pupils in the field, it became apparent that the act was a significant departure from that passed in 1944. Importantly it embraced an *educational* rather than a nurture intention for the subject, enshrining this within a general requirement that the whole curriculum should 'promote the spiritual, moral, cultural, mental and physical development of pupils at the school and of society'. No longer was RE to 'teach religion' but to teach *about* religion. This was to be its proper educational task, the study of religious traditions. Whilst the act stated that the locally agreed syllabuses should, 'reflect the fact that the religious traditions in Great Britain are in the main Christian', a 'fact' which perhaps existed more powerfully in the minds of some protagonists in the great debate than in social reality as we have seen, it went on to say that the teaching and practices of the other principal religions represented in the country must also be taught. Despite the ongoing confusion of RE with what was termed 'collective worship' in the act, and later attempts by the department of education to reintroduce a more restrictive interpretation of the subject (the infamous Circular 1/94), the 1988 act laid a workable foundation for the new 'world religions' approach to RE which had been pioneered by institutions such as Lancaster University, and nurtured by the Religious Education Council, the Shap conferences and publications such as The British Journal of Religious Education.

What, then, is contemporary RE or, as it is also now called, Religious Studies? Comparison of the new (1997) Cambridgeshire agreed syllabus with the previous 1949 version quoted above shows how things have changed. The section on the aims of RE understands that religion is a significant element of human experience, that it is therefore the job of the subject to help pupils acquire knowledge and understanding of Christianity and other religions and how these influence the beliefs, values and traditions of individuals, communities, societies and cultures. It speaks about developing the ability to explore, reflect on and respond to human experience and make reasoned and informed responses to religious and moral issues. Its approach is investigative, open, challenging and empathetic. It takes for granted that we are 'living in a society of diverse religions and cultures' and that RE should both raise pupils' consciousness about their own assumptions and beliefs whilst also drawing them into respect for the religious lives of others. Carefully designed, the syllabus provides detailed guidance to teachers on the world religions content of modern RE shaped to suit students in every Key Stage. Splitting this thematically under headings such as 'writings', 'worship', 'festivals and fasts', 'self and community', it examines with increasing sophistication each of the six major world faith traditions so that by the end of their school life pupils should have a well-developed knowledge and understanding of these religions.

RE such as that promoted by the Cambridgeshire and other recent syllabuses is a subject which possesses academic clout, one which can only properly be delivered by specialist teachers fully qualified in this field, whose own personal religious commitment might perhaps be a useful resource but is certainly not a prerequisite for excellence. In common with all the other Humanities subjects it seeks to enthuse pupils about its content, not only by teaching the myriad of hard facts intrinsic to it but also by initiating them imaginatively into the fascinating world of thought and behaviour characteristic of Hindus, Christians or Sikhs. To do this it uses the whole panoply of modern educational methodology, but especially visits to religious buildings and communities, exploration of visual imagery and artefacts, religious art, dance and music, role play and group work, debates and structured discussion, use of IT, videos, religious texts and so on and on. Pupils are encouraged to do GCSE and A levels, whilst in higher education the range of religious studies options is staggering, as is the number and variety of books which have been rolling off the presses in ever-increasing numbers to enrich learning and underpin the subject's success.

We have been invited to dream some dreams for the 21st century, a reflective process as crucial for RE's future as it is for all the other topics discussed in chapters here. Those involved during this century with the formation and delivery of the subject have sometimes, as we have seen, allowed their dreaming to run riot and to blot out some uncomfortable realities. This is why future visions need to be firmly rooted in what has been discussed above — the history of RE's development and the social context in which the subject operates. What questions and directions does such an analysis suggest?

What has to be remembered first of all about RE in state schools is that it is hedged in by certain parameters, governed by such mundane matters as legal requirements, money, staff training and availability and the pressures of the school curriculum — RE is normally allowed at most a mere 5% of time per week. It also has its shape defined by the various claims made upon it by government, academe and the faith communities themselves; all bid for ownership of its content and purposes.

Law dictates that the subject must follow certain generally laid down criteria (see above). Simultaneously it hands the detail of specific content to locally formed SACREs (Standing Advisory Committees) charged with the duty of producing *locally* agreed syllabuses representing the views of county councillors, teachers, the Church of England and all the other faith groups of the region. Politicians and government agencies, however, dreaming of common values and national identity, often long for more direct control and are drawn into producing model *national* curricula and subject 'cores' (see SCAA documents). Specialists have their own axes to grind. Generally espousing liberal educational values and believing that all religions offer paths to the truth, they are of the opinion that these can be well, if not better, taught by those who do not adhere to them but rather are able to stand back, combining an enthusiastically sympathetic approach with a degree of detachment. Some religious communities, e.g. within Christianity, Judaism or Hinduism embrace this approach with ease, their representatives feeling at home round the SACRE table in county halls! Others, however, of a more conservative or orthodox character, hold understandings of their own faiths which do not fit comfortably into this collaborative mould. They lean towards a solution which would remove either religious education (or their own offspring) from the state sector altogether and make it the governing ethos of distinctive religious schools. This solution is complicated by the existence already of religious schools maintained largely by the state (C of E, Jewish and Muslim) and by Humanists and some on the political Left who take common cause with the religiously conservative, also arguing that RE has no place in any national education system.

The RE of the future will have to cope with all these parameters and conflicting pressures. It will also have to keep its nerve, however! If the subject is to be true to itself and do its job properly it will have to go on being thoroughly responsive to the changing realities of religion and society, not only in Britain but globally, in order to stimulate an internal debate about the nature of both its content and aims. The subject's intrinsic character which is open, exploratory, questioning and analytical, together with the fact of its local determination, will ensure that it is shaped by a genuine dialogue with religious traditions and world views both at popular, community level and in the field of academic scholarship. This will inevitably challenge established patterns and pose questions. For example, are the six world religions which presently form RE's content out-of-date meta-narratives, inappropriate subject matter for a post-modern world? Should RE deal instead with the 'world views' which really shape the lives of people, especially the majority in the West — humanism, socialism, nationalism, consumerism, rationalism? Or should it delve into the mysteries and concerns of the New Age? Or, capitalising on its humane and empathetic qualities, confront existential questions and those key debates about morality which affect the world's destiny — war and peace, poverty, environment, racial hatred, issues of sexuality? Such concerns about the subject are already being voiced in recent copies of the profession's *British Journal of Religious Education* under article headings such as, 'Should RE Foster National Consciousness?', 'Paganism in the Classroom' (how to teach it) and 'Belief in God in Britain 1945-1996: Moving the Scenery Behind Classroom RE'. Very similar discussions are pursued in *RE Features* (1998). Both publications combine questioning of RE's content for the future with speculation on the thornier topic of what its aims might be — though naturally the two are closely related.

RE has not abandoned aims that are wider than the purely educational objectives enumerated, as we have seen, in the most recent Cambridgeshire syllabus. Even these push the subject out beyond the confines of the classroom into the personal lives of individual pupils and into hopes for a better society. This is dangerous ground since RE's previous forays into these areas have often come to grief and seen fantasy triumph over reality. There is a need to tread with care but the subject and its protagonists still entertain hopes that its educative impact will be felt in the future, firstly in its capacity to influence the spiritual and moral growth of persons, what the Brazilian educationalist Paulo Freire has called 'conscientisation' or 'education for liberation' (see BJRE, vol. 20.3, Summer 1998). Here the subject can draw from the deep well of the religious traditions, their insights into the nature and condition of humanity, the complexities of morality and the meaning and purpose of life in the concrete circumstances of the present. These traditions challenge pupils to examine deeply who they are, what they believe, why and what consequences flow from such convictions. In this sense RE, demanding personal response, aims to be life changing.

Secondly, future visions of the subject's purpose very much emphasise its potential as a means of promoting a more just and harmonious society. The religiously educated person, properly knowledgeable about and sympathetic towards religions in Britain, and prompted to be self-questioningly aware, is an agent of social transformation and so plays a crucial role in the creation of this society. RE hopes to grow such individuals, but another means to the same end is for it to draw attention to those common teachings which unite religions in critique of questionable values characteristic of modernity, e.g. its overweening materialism, xenophobia or individualism, an alternative message which proclaims welcome to the stranger, condemnation of the lust for wealth and prophetically calls for a social order founded on loving relationships. Furthermore, RE's contribution to the building of a better society is, ultimately, that the subject itself models what it hopes to achieve, embracing and functioning on multicultural assumptions about the nature of British society and operating at every level through dialogue, real conversation, with religious traditions. One contributor to *RE Futures* speaks of the 'I-Thou relationship' which the subject nurtures between pupils and teacher. It is this respectful bond which is replicated in RE's attitude to the 'objects' of its study — the faiths themselves. So it feels at home with the approach and intentions of organisations such as the Inter-Faith Network and sees its future mission as the fostering of what John Habgood has described as 'critical solidarity'. This functions both in terms of individuals and for society. It means that RE must seek to avoid 'confessionalism' which attempts to convert both to a particular religion, and 'essentialism' which merges all distinction into one amorphous melting pot. Rather, the challenge for RE is to help form a society which can simultaneously guard and honour the special, unique character of each faith, celebrating diversity, whilst also contributing to the construction of a framework of mutually acceptable values which may bind society together:

> 'The challenge facing everyone ... is to evolve the common visions and structures necessary for sustaining an integrated but richly diverse community, without either assimilation or fragmentation.' (*Religions in the UK* (1997), p. 46)

This is the tension of unity with diversity. RE's task for the future is to forge a 'critical solidarity' which builds community whilst promoting healthy debate of every faith claim and ethic — especially in the light of conflicts in places such as the Balkans, critiquing those which purvey sectarian, nationalistic or fundamentalist, 'closed' world views. It must engage individuals and society in a continuing dialogue which is at root about truth itself and how we are all to live this out together in the century to come.

BIBLIOGRAPHY

British Journal of Religious Education (BJRE), Christian Education Movement

S. Bruce, *Religion in Modern Britain* (OUP, 1995)

R. Goldman, *New Society*, 27 May 1965, p. 10

G. Parsons, *What are we in Britain? Defining the Context of Religious Education for the 21st Century*, Conference address to 1995 conference of the association of Religious Education inspectors, advisors and consultants

RE Futures: A Reader in Religious Education (PCfRE, 1998)

Religions in the UK: A Multi-Faith Directory (University of Derby and the Inter-Faith Network, 1997)

School Curriculum and Assessment Authority; Model Syllabuses, 1994

QUESTIONS

1 What role, if any, might the churches have to play in the Religious Education of the future?

2 What should be RE's content in the 21st century?

3 Are the aims of RE described above realistic?

4 Is RE central or superfluous in the curriculum of state schools?

The Heart of the Stranger

Anne Krisman

WE ARE children of many traditions — inheritors of shared wisdom and tragic misunderstandings, of proud hopes and humble successes. In that which we share, let us see the common prayer of humanity; in that which we differ, let us wonder at the freedom of man; in our unity and in our differences, let us know the uniqueness that is God. (taken from Reform Synagogues of Great Britain Prayer for Inter-faith meetings)

A HOME FOR ALL THE RELIGIONS

Take a glimpse into my world. Here is my classroom and all around are images of the faiths. Guru Nanak looks down on us, there is a Franciscan cross, a golden Buddha, an Indian wedding hat that Micky's dad rescued from a skip. Some old family Bibles with yellowing pages, velvety pictures of Mecca, a cover for cholla, a mirrored picture of Krishna playing his flute, holy water from Lourdes. Together, we have built a room that resonates with the diversity of life, a place that a Sikh boy calls 'a home for all the religions'.

And here we are, the 16+ RE group, sitting together in a circle. A Jewish teacher and the four pupils who have the greatest difficulties in our special needs school. Yet it is the group that is the most instinctive about religion and human experience.

Peter has just said something that has touched us all, 'I feel like I am in a dark tunnel'. His nan has died and the others try to comfort him. Shazia, who is a Muslim, says, 'You should be happy, your nan is in Paradise'. Pooneet, who is a Hindu devotee of Sathya Sai Baba, sings a bhajan (devotional song) very sweetly, 'We surrender to love'. Abdulla, a Muslim, asks if he can make tea for us all.

Peter suddenly gets up and walks over to what we call our peace windows — the windows of the classroom that look out onto fields, trees and flowers. We follow him. 'I feel better now', he says, after gazing out for a while. Why is inter-faith so easy in this context, a special school for pupils with learning difficulties? Why is it that we seem to have found an understanding between us, that often goes beyond words? Perhaps it is because we are a ready made community, that we are united in our difficulties. Perhaps it is because intellect can blur the simplest understandings and we can go straight to the core of the matter. We do not see our different faiths as a barrier, but as a way of helping each other through the hard times in life.

UNDERSTANDING WHAT PEOPLE ARE

I share with you the experiences of my special needs school as I feel we have touched the essence of inter-faith — about understanding the 'heart of the stranger'. It is one important step to learn facts about different faiths, to visit places of worship, to witness others' religious ceremonies. But the inter-faith journey for me is also about what people are, above and beyond what they do.

TO BE A JEWISH WOMAN

As a Jewish woman this theme is central. I am more than what I do when I go to synagogue. Deep within me is the Jewish collective memory of dispersion and rootlessness, the desire for justice and equality, the hope for peace and unity.

The poet Emmanuel Eydoux writes of the Jewish experience:

> to look when others turn away...
> to continue the struggle even when one is not the strongest
>
> to cry out when others keep silent...
>
> and to remember when others have forgotten.

My parents brought me up in the mainstream Orthodox tradition. I made the decision to change to the Reform synagogue movement when I heard the rabbi, Henry Goldstein, give a brave sermon about racial attacks that had happened in the black community. This was at Yom Kippur, when many ministers hammer home the importance of in-marriage and Jewish education to a guaranteed large attendance!

The sermon pointed me in the right direction. I understood that having a social conscience and a Jewish heart were one and the same.

INTO THE MILLENNIUM

What themes will there be in inter-faith work into the millennium? I have chosen some areas that fascinate me; I know you will have your own.

Recognising diversity

Our fixed boundaries for defining religions may need to be re-defined. We can no longer say that all Sikhs wear the 5Ks or that all Jews keep kosher. Within the Jewish community there are many people who see themselves as strongly 'culturally Jewish', defining their identity through family, community, food, and music, rather than through Torah study or Israel.

I teach a girl who is both a Hindu and a Sikh, whose family has built a home shrine in an old bathroom. The shrine is bursting with bright images of Hindu gods, side by side with pictures of the gurus. 'Sikhism came from Hinduism', she tells me, 'It is all one'. There is a continuing need to go into the community and speak to believers about how they live their lives.

We will need to learn more about how nationality shapes religious identity — Pakistani, Turkish and Somali Muslims, for example, will be linked by a common religion, yet will be culturally distinctive. I was surprised when I attended a local synagogue for Jewish people from India, Israel, Iran and Iraq. The women wore saris and the atmosphere was far warmer and livelier than the sedate services I was used to. I realised that synagogues in Britain have reflected elements of church worship in their order and ritual, and that it was wrong to assume that this was the norm for every strand of Judaism.

Religions cannot be divorced from their cultural context. The same is true for Christianity; when I look for images of Jesus to show my pupils, it is difficult to find pictures that reflect him as a Jewish Palestinian of the 1st century. Blonde hair and blue-eyed images prevail.

Many people think of Christianity as synonymous with English people, yet there are also Chinese, Pakistani and African Christians whose expression of Christianity reflects their nationality and culture. I am delighted to see that recent schools Religious Education broadcasts are beginning to reflect the many ways of being Christian in today's society.

Communities

My formative time in inter-faith work was with the Manor Park Faith in Community project. Here was a vibrantly religious community within an area of high poverty and unemployment. There was much valuable work to be done building bridges between faiths, working with refugees and fighting racism.

I am now involved in a middle-class community, where the emphasis is different. My Jewish friend, who is a teacher, has neighbours who are Sikhs and Hindus. They are all professionals, settled in this country for many years. Like the local Jewish community they have made the move from the poorer parts of East London to the more affluent suburbs.

What will inter-faith be for in communities that appear to be integrated? Will we stay in our 'patch', working in our local Council of Faiths group, or will we be linked nationally or even within Europe, helped by new technology? This may seem fanciful, but my pupils now communicate with children with learning difficulties in Canada, South Africa and USA through the Internet, sharing their hopes and thoughts about life.

Language

I remember attending a Religious Education seminar where the predominantly Christian audience was asked to share their memories of a time when they experienced a deep spirituality. As each person shared their insight I was conscious that almost each one included a solitary response to nature. A time spent climbing a mountain, a sense of complete isolation on a deserted beach, a moment of contemplation in a forest. I realised that I felt differently. My own spirituality, as a Jewish woman, was more linked with the energy of being with people.

My hopes for inter-faith into the millennium is that we will begin to look more closely at the ways in which our cultural and linguistic understandings differ. We need to explore key concepts within religions — spirituality, justice, service, compassion, suffering, love — to see if we are speaking the same language.

A word like 'forgiveness' may have different resonances for a Jew, for example, than a Christian. The late Rabbi Hugo Gryn spoke powerfully about the Jewish understanding of forgiveness after the Holocaust, explaining that he could not 'stand on the street corner dispensing forgiveness', and that it was not his responsibility to forgive the perpetrators, especially as they never accepted their guilt themselves.

Education

In a controversial move, Rabbi Jonathan Wittenberg has advocated the setting up of a multi-faith school which would place importance on religious traditions and values, and where pupils would learn 'that there are many paths through life to God'. He has stated, 'We must inculcate tolerance of each other's faiths, while anchoring our children firmly in the practice and wisdom of their own'.

Rabbi Wittenberg's vision is contradicted by the growing pressure for religious schools. How will this affect the inter-faith agenda? Will pupils be educated about other faiths in a sensitive way — or will this not be seen as a priority?

Social issues

Rabbi Leo Baeck (1873–1956) has stated, 'When we are approached by a human being demanding his right, we cannot replace definite ethical action by mere vague goodwill'. I have spoken of the need to look within our communities to understand the evolving traditions of people with whom we work, and to explore the differences that we have in our religious language and concepts. Yet we must also look outwards, to larger issues where campaigning can make a difference; to ending the Third World Debt, to fighting racism and nationalism and negative images of Islam in the media.

CONCLUSION

I have a collection of holy books on the table, a small Torah scroll, the Quran, the Bible. 'What do they have in common?' I ask. The class starts calling out, 'Love! Peace! Respect! Understanding between different religions!' I sit down, a little stunned. A group of special needs pupils have got to the heart of the matter. The rest is commentary.

NOTES

Quotations are taken from Forms of Prayer for Jewish Worship (Daily, Sabbath and Occasional Prayers), published by Reform synagogues of Great Britain, 1977.

Rabbi Hugo Gryn's interview, 'What happened to the Man at Auschwitz' can be read on http//:www.worth.org.uk/identity/auschwitz.htm

'Have Faith in Sharing', an article in *The Times Educational Supplement* by Jonathan Wittenberg, 5.2.99

When the Babylonian Hillel was asked to explain Judaism while standing on one foot, he said, 'Do not do to others that which is hurtful to you. The rest is commentary'.

QUESTIONS

1 If you had to draw a symbol for inter-faith work into the new millennium, what would it be? What images would you use to convey the spirit of inter-faith?

2 The writer makes a distinction between what someone is and what someone does. Is this a fair distinction? Make two lists for yourself that include the two ideas and share these with the group.

3 If inter-faith is difficult and you have reservations about it, what hopes are there for living harmoniously in our culturally and religiously diverse world?

Claim Oikoumene, Reject Divisiveness

Walter Schenk

Ironically, it was nearly a month to the day from the outset of what had become the daily routine of NATO's bombing of Yugoslavia that two alienated and disaffected young high school students in Colorado decided the time had come to unleash violence of their own design. So intense and deeply rooted was their hatred that they had taken over a full year to devise and implement their plan to take the ultimate revenge against their fellow classmates and teachers.

In the wake of their violent and bloody rampage 15 students, including the two young men themselves and one teacher were killed by their gunfire. Mercifully, the more than 50 bombs that they had constructed, armed and either placed or tossed around the school did not go off. A diary discovered in the days after this tragic event revealed that the two had nurtured their hatred with a fascination of Nazi Germany, a predilection for the use of fascist phrases in German, as well as an attraction to neo-Nazi music and politics. The diary also detailed their plans to kill the 'jocks', school athletes who with their friends humiliated and even physically abused them, as well as Blacks and Jews.

On the Sunday immediately following this horrific event, US Vice-President Al Gore travelled to Littleton, Colorado to join with 70,000 grieving citizens and parents gathered in the rain for a memorial service. Standing before them, even while missiles were coursing toward their targets in Yugoslavia, he declared, 'Parents, we can stop the violence and hate. In a culture rife with violence, where too many people place too little value on human life, we can rise up and say, 'No More!'

During that very same week a group calling themselves the White Wolves set off a bomb in South London's Brixton neighbourhood. According to reports, no one was seriously injured. Then, exactly one week later still another bomb was exploded in the Brick Lane neighbourhood near to the City of London financial market. According to reports, over 30 persons were injured. This time another group calling themselves Combat 18 took responsibility. Prime Minister Tony Blair, while attending the 50th Anniversary celebration of NATO in Washington, DC, immediately condemned the attacks as 'outrageous'. He went on to say, 'the Government will make every effort to find out who was responsible and bring them to justice'.

Police investigators informed the public that organisers of Combat 18 had apparently contrived their name by way of an oblique reference to Adolph Hitler's name. The letters A and H are numbered 1 and 8 in the alphabet. The White Wolves, they tell us, were formed as a splinter group of Combat 18 declaring ominously that the White Wolves will howl as the new millennium dawns. Both groups stated that their goal is to clear Britain of non-whites, Jews and other minorities.

On the occasion of the second bombing many noted the timed interval of the two bombings and expressed concern that the bombings may become a weekly routine. Both neighbourhoods are home to racial and ethnic minorities. Both bombings were apparently carried out by extremist right-wing organisations. And then on the next Friday evening as this article was being completed those fears were tragically fulfilled. Another bomb was set off in London, this time in a gay bar in the West End. The first reports received indicated that many had been seriously injured.

Was it mere coincidence that these awful events occurred simultaneously on both sides of the Atlantic? Evidently it was not. These tragic events are clearly drawn together by their common attraction to the neo-Nazi movement. Both in America and in Britain these actions were obviously scheduled to mark Hitler's birthday, 20 April, a point made in the diaries of the gunmen in Colorado.

Meanwhile in Yugoslavia, NATO was engaged in an all-out air war to hobble the ability of the Milosevic ethno-centric government from further 'cleansing' ethnic Albanians from the Yugoslavian province of Kosovo. Yet again we find ourselves caught on the cusp of irony as NATO's bombing immediately only aided and abetted the Milosevic objectives by forcing hundreds of thousands of Albanians to flee their homes in Kosovo and other parts of Yugoslavia. As refugees streamed across the borders of Yugoslavia into neighbouring countries, one of the worst humanitarian disasters in modern history had been created. Clearly, not one of NATO's military planners realised the massive numbers of refugees that would be created by their actions. At a press conference in Washington, DC, during the week following, a State Department spokesperson was asked if the use of violence simply created increased violence. His response? 'This is not a philosophy class; this is a State Department briefing, we are here to discuss the prosecution of the President's foreign policy.'

In these transitional months between the old millennium and the new, people of faith live as we always have lived: eschatologically. We live as always, between the 'no longer' and the 'not yet'. We find ourselves called to give up the old even before we can know the new. And, if US State Department briefings are not permitted to be an appropriate arena for the discussion of moral and ethical issues which confront the world community, then perhaps that notion of reality and others need to be challenged forthwith.

In such moments as these we are confronted again both with the reality of our human condition and with a choice. Will we succumb to the 'realities' of the present age, giving ourselves over passively to the authority of the Principalities and Powers? Or will we decide to live under the authority of the One who incarnated the possibility of transformation which effects reconciliation and justice within human community, heals the breaches which lead us into war with one another and with ourselves?

When people of faith are confronted with the challenges and opportunities of a new millennium, it is useful to consider the witness of the faithful who have struggled with these issues before us. Yet as we look to the witnesses in Scripture we must be clear that we do not so much search for answers, as we seek a re-grounding in God's word, guidance and insight into God's will for the world and God's intention for God's people.

False divisions of enmity have emerged before. This was the world in which Jesus began his ministry. Fractious divisions and hostilities are laced all through the background of the New Testament. Woven into the fabric of Luke's account of Jesus' mission and ministry are important dimensions of 1st century social and historical life which can be easily overlooked by those of us who read it at an historical distance. Just as easily as one who reads a newspaper account of the London bombings might not catch the common significance of the Brixton, Brick Lane and Soho neighbourhoods which link them together ominously, we may gloss over similar references in biblical accounts. Yet once one is aware that these are neighbourhoods in which racial and ethnic and sexual minorities live, the significance and importance of that social context cannot be avoided.

Luke tells how Jesus persistently and intentionally addressed the reality of social, class, and political divisions within society. For the people who heard Jesus' teaching, what he taught about dismantling and disempowering of false barriers within their world was what was 'good' about the *good* news. Luke's view of Jesus' teaching was a radically universal gospel message that was wrapped up in and fully expressed in his life, death and resurrection. The gospel Jesus taught claimed to be for the Oikoumene, radically open for the whole-inhabited earth. At the same time he rejected as false parochial distinctions and hostile barriers within human community.

This meaning emerges in Luke's description of those who were drawn to Jesus simply to be in his presence, to be taught by him and to be healed by him. This theme is found early on in Luke when he included the story of the shepherds (Luke 2:8-20) in his birth narrative. The first announcement of the good news by the angels of God was to poor shepherds who lived in the fields.

It was also the point of a subsequent story which Luke included about the outset of Jesus' ministry (Luke 4:14–30) immediately following his experience in the wilderness. Having been grounded in the Spirit, Jesus returned to Galilee to teach. All went well until he returned to Nazareth. Once there he entered the synagogue where he had the audacity to point out to the elders that God's ultimate concern extends to the whole human community. He reminded them that it was during a severe famine that God had sent Elijah not to any of the widows starving in Israel, but to a gentile widow in the far-off city of Zarephath in Sidon. The elders found Jesus' teaching of God's universal love for all people so unwelcome and offensive that they became enraged and ran their heretofore favourite son out of his own hometown.

Nevertheless, Luke makes the point again for the fourth time. He tells how great multitudes came to hear Jesus teach (Luke 6:17–19) not only from all the agreeable areas of Judea and Jerusalem, *but also from the less than acceptable gentile regions of Tyre and Sidon in Phoenicia*. The crowds just came from *everywhere*. The scandal was of course that *everyone from everywhere* was welcome; no one was turned away.

From Luke's perspective Jesus launched his public ministry by directly rejecting the Systems of Domination, those powerful forces that maintain the lines of separation that falsely divide peoples and persons over against one another. For those who first heard his message, the *good* news was that his message was addressed to the Oikoumene, the whole-inhabited world: no divisions, no exceptions.

It must have been truly extraordinary; yes, even scandalous. No social or economic class, no racial or ethnic groups, no national or political group, no gender, no religious group was excluded. Jesus addressed his ministry of teaching and healing to all people.

He commenced his teaching by setting out stark contrasts, first moving through four blessings and then through four woes. It was much like a 1st-century version of our contemporary litanies of good news/bad news:

> Well, the good news is:
> That the poor by way of their experience
> are prepared to experience the Reign of God now.
> But the bad news is:
> That the rich already have their comfort.
> Well, the good news is:
> That those who are hungry now will be filled up.
> But the bad news is:
> That those who are full now will be hungry.
> Well, the good news is:
> That those who are sorrowful now will be filled with joy.

But the bad news is:
That those who are laughing now will mourn and weep.
Well, the good news is:
That those who have been rejected and hated now because they have associated themselves with Jesus and his heretical, offensive teachings that the Reign of God is among the Oikoumene will have many opportunities to celebrate.
But the bad news is:
That those who have been so concerned about maintaining their good reputations ought to remember that they share ignominious company with false prophets!

One can plainly see that Jesus had apparently passed over what must have been the common wisdom in his day as it is in ours: preachers ought to avoid controversy in their first sermon; it might turn the flock off. Jesus set out his radical message of the universality of God's grace all at the beginning. He opened his ministry not with entertaining stories to put people at ease, but with a salvo over the bow of the Domination System itself, the entrenched system maintained by the Powers That Be that militate to keep the power arrangements in society just the way they are.

Peter Stienfels, religion editor of the *New York Times*, recently reviewed *The Crisis in the Churches*, the newly published book of Princeton University sociologist, Robert Wuthnow. Wuthnow argues that the presenting symptom of the crisis is financial, observing that the American church has fallen on hard times even as the American economy has roared ahead unabated. He wonders: if 80% of the church's family incomes are middle class, then why hasn't the church benefited from this increased income? So, he reckons, if the money isn't getting into the church's coffers the root of the crisis must be a 'spiritual malaise!'

But Wuthnow also observes with some concern that the American church also seems to want it both ways. He notes that while we are troubled by the spread of poverty throughout the world, it also esteems wealth. He laments that church leadership seems to know little about economic matters with the possible exception of church finances. So while he hears much talk about tithing, much of it seems to be self-serving as there is next to no commentary from church leadership on the ethical issues involved in making decisions on the distribution and handling of the larger, remaining balance of church members' income. He says that when clergy do comment on questions of work and money they usually couch it in terms of personal fulfilment and individual happiness: 'You've worked hard for that; you deserve it.'

It may be that Wuthnow has inadvertently become part of the problem he has rightfully identified. His working definition of 'middle income' seems to be somewhat over-broad since it reaches down to annual incomes of only $20,000 for a family of four. This is, however, only $3,950 away from the official so-called 'poverty line' set by the government for 1997.

On the other hand, for approximately 30 years the thriving American economy has only benefited the top 5% of American households, which make $188,828 per year. Between 1989 and 1995 those incomes have increased by 11%. But the lower four-fifths of the population have lost ground; and the lowest 20% of households that make only $8,350 in annual income have *actually lost over 3%*.

Meanwhile, corporate use of part-time workers to avoid paying full-time wages with full medical and pension benefits has dramatically increased. Likewise, business and other sectors have also increased reliance on so-called 'out-sourcing' practices. Here portions of work previously done in-house are contracted out to other companies that use low-paid temporary and part-time workers.

There have often been various attempts to put a different spin or interpretation on the words of Jesus to make his teaching about the poor and hungry more palatable and perhaps less offensive. These attempts to 'spiritualise' the teaching of Jesus serve only to extract them from the context of the real world so as not to trouble our sensibilities. They make the poor into the emotionally depressed or humbled, or the hungry into those who are eager for good things to happen to good people.

The former Mayor of New York City, Ed Koch, made quite a name for himself coining typically New York aphorisms. The one that actually ended up on official 'No Parking' signs which were installed during his administration was, 'Don't Even Think About Parking Here'. Well, Luke's witness seems to be quite similar: Don't even think about spiritualising Jesus' Blessings and Woes. Luke made Jesus teaching clear that under the Reign of God the present world order was being overturned, now, and that people of faith are called to live in and under that Reality. Don't even think that Jesus taught anything less than that!

With these Blessings and Woes Jesus defined the distinctive contours of the message he personified. With them he systematically repudiated the Principalities and Powers that struggle to hold sway over this world. The gospel that Jesus taught and lived championed radical social and economic equality *because* these *inequities* form the foundation of the Domination System itself.

Jesus knew that human exploitation is built on power acquired by accumulated wealth. It hinders the movement of the Reign of God among God's people. Remember at the outset of his gospel how Luke led his readers in recollecting the song which Mary sang to Elizabeth (Luke 1:46-55) after Mary realised she was pregnant? The church has called her words the Magnificat.

Mary sang:

> My *soul* magnifies the Lord,
> and my *spirit* rejoices in God my Saviour
> For he has looked with favour on the lowliness of his servant.
> Surely, from now on all generations will call me blessed;
> ... His mercy is for those who fear him ...
> ... he has scattered the proud in the imaginations of their hearts;
> He has brought down the powerful from their thrones,
> and lifted up the lowly;
> He has filled the hungry with good things,
> and sent the rich away empty.

The Blessings and Woes that Jesus used to introduce his sermon to the masses, to the common people, paralleled directly this Vision of Mary. For it was her remarkable vision that foresaw a new future in a New Age under the Reign of God.

Now, Jesus declared it plainly: the old order is being overturned. The faithful are called to actively resist being seduced by the Principalities and Powers that put peoples and persons over against each other. No longer will these Powers That Be have the power to beguile the faithful, tricking us with false notions that somehow economic and social upward mobility for the rich is somehow the expression of God's generosity.

These false notions not only exploit the poor, they also serve to create the poor. No longer can the Principalities and Powers deceive the faithful with clever ideas that our salvation is somehow derived from the satisfaction in knowing that one's income level has now attained a certain number of digits, or in the pride that one has amassed a certain amount of wealth.

For the people of the Beatitudes, these things count for very little. The point of Jesus' Blessings is that the poor can see the Reign of God clearly *because* they are not distracted by excess wealth. Jesus blessed and sided with the poor, *not* because of any misguided notion that the poor were somehow morally virtuous. But rather, he sided with them *because of their suffering*.

The poor were blessed, not because poverty was somehow a holy condition to which all should aspire, but *because they suffer*. The gift they have acquired by way of their undeserved suffering provides them with a unique perspective to see things the way they are. From their viewpoint they see the System of Domination and the Reign of God with clarity, without the various encumbrances and seductions of accumulated wealth.

The gospel of Jesus is a call to all to live by faith between the times, between the 'no longer' and the 'not yet'. Yet this kind of living will usually mean being associated with those who are perceived by the world as those who espouse crazy notions and do crazy things. People who are committed to a world where there are no dividing lines to keep persons and peoples from one another. People who are committed to a world where,

> the proud have been scattered in the imaginations of their hearts; where the powerful have been brought down from their thrones, where the lowly have been lifted up; where the hungry have been filled with good things, and the rich have been sent away empty.

More often than not, the faithful find themselves in the company of such crazy 'heretics' and others who do not buy the accepted values of the larger world.

Those who hear Jesus' good news will most always find themselves standing over against the established order, not because they count on getting a blessing in return, but because that is where their faithfulness and commitment to Jesus has led them. And that, as we know, is a very dangerous but nevertheless blessed place indeed.

QUESTIONS

1 What does it mean for people of faith to live eschatologically today, to live 'between the times' as we cross into a new millennium? What are the issues facing us as individual Christians and as the Church?

2 How will people of faith claim the Oikoumene for God in the new millennium, while rejecting divisiveness within human community?

3 Re-reading Luke 1:46-55, restate Mary's song using your own contemporary references and illustrations. How does her song inform our vocation to faithful living?

Apologetics — A Discipline Whose Time Has Come

Mervyn Willshaw

VIVIAN GREEN in his *New History of Christianity* sees two dangers confronting the churches as they move towards the new millennium. The first is that they become increasingly sectarian, clusters of believers in an unbelieving world from which they have become isolated, fundamentalist in theological outlook and moral stance. The second is that they may

> 'adapt further to meet the needs of an ever-changing society, becoming increasingly immersed in secular culture, both in terms of doctrine and morals, shedding to a greater or lesser extent their supernatural framework.'[1]

Others are even more pessimistic. John Kent thinks that religion is far from withering away but that the 'Western religious creativity no longer works happily with orthodox Christian symbols'.

The religiously-minded grapple now with ideas of impersonal theism which take little account of older Western ideas about God. He adds chillingly, 'The barbarians have arrived, twilight has descended, and this time when it lifts the Western churches will probably have ceased to function...'.[2]

Don Cupitt goes further. For him, it is not only Christian symbols which have ceased to be credible. There is now no room for any belief in the supernatural nor can we any longer speak of public truth. Everything is relative.

'The position is that there are no absolutes or fixed intelligible essences, able to hold at least a few of our linguistic meanings steady.'[3]

> 'Everything has a history. Linguistic meanings have histories, truth has a history, morality has a history, religious belief has a history, reason itself has a history. And of course the doctrine that everything has a history itself has a history. Result? Universal meltdown, nihilism, postmodernism.'[4]

It would be easy to dismiss such assessments as inappropriate in a volume of essays on millennium opportunities. After a century of church decline the faithful need cheering up. Things have been bad before but God is the same, yesterday, today and forever. So let us not give way to gloom. The God of Moses, Nehemiah and Jesus can be trusted to astound a few dreary theologians and historians.

But that would be to offer false comfort, to reveal a profound lack of faith and, in the end, to dishonour God. For in all the intellectual effort and upheaval that has given rise to the contemporary situation, the Spirit of God has surely been at work, if indeed this is God's world.

CHALLENGES TO FAITH

The present climate of thought has been a long time in the making. The dawn of the Enlightenment, with its stress upon rationality and toleration, represented a major challenge to Christianity. Traditional reliance on miracles, revelation and the inspiration of Scripture as evidences for the truth of the Christian faith was questioned. The growth of modern science gradually led to the rise of naturalism. Trust in authority as the way to knowledge was replaced by reliance upon experience and observation. The story of geology in the 19th century illustrates the change. Few of those involved in the development of this new science were avowed enemies of the Christian religion. The occupants of the new chairs in Oxford and Cambridge were, of course, clergymen of the Church of England. Sir Charles Lyell, the father of modern geology, though not ordained, remained a practising Anglican all his life. A cautious man, not naturally given to rocking the boat of faith, his scientific integrity nevertheless forced him to move from belief in catastrophes such as the Flood as agents of geological change to the recognition that the earth had come to be as he found it through gradual evolutionary processes over vast ages of time.

The success of science generated an epistemology in which empiricism was seen as the only way to knowledge and meaning.

It also led to a deterministic approach to life. For all Darwin's stress on randomness and natural selection in the evolutionary process, there seemed to many to be a degree of inevitability about it. It suggested impersonal and inexorable forces in nature outside the control of human beings and independent of the influence of God. In biology Watson and Crick were to push this determinism to its limits in this century, but the same approach was found in other disciplines too. Freud used it in psychology and altered for all time our understanding of what it is to be human. The discovery of the unconscious forces shaping personality from earliest infancy undermined romantic notions about human freedom and autonomy. Marx found the same inevitability in our economic and political life. He dedicated *Das Kapital* to Charles Darwin.

It was much less easy to see the image of God in human beings after these things than it had been earlier. We were now too much a part of the physical and animal creation to be a special creation and there were serious implications for our understanding of the person of Jesus.

In all this the divine inspiration of the Bible began to look shaky. The early chapters of Genesis were not to be trusted as history or science.

Colenso's Zulus opened his eyes to moral enormities in the Old Testament and his own careful reading exposed factual absurdities. Strauss found 'myth' in the New Testament as well as the Old. More sober scholars could not overlook questions about the historicity, authorship and integrity of individual books. The understanding of biblical authority and inspiration simply had to change.

In 1901 Ernst Troeltsch in his *Absoluteness of Christianity* insisted that the Christian religion must be interpreted in the context of cultural history because 'the original naive certainty held by every existing type of culture and value system regarding the obviousness of its own validity has been shaken.'[5] In an earlier work he had written, 'All historical happening is knit together in a permanent correlation... Any one event is related to all others. Therefore the historical and the relative are identical'.[6]

Now he made clear that the Christian religion, like all religions, is a historical phenomenon and, therefore, a relative phenomenon. The absoluteness of Christianity will be discovered not through naive dogmatism but through a process of comparative evaluation. The criterion of evaluation is something which will emerge from the religion which is strongest and most profound. Troeltsch himself was convinced that Christianity remains the highest of religions. It must be understood as the culmination point and convergence point of all developmental tendencies in religion. But there is no guarantee that it will always remain the final culmination point. It cannot, and must not, be regarded as an absolute, perfect, immutable truth.

Increasing exposure to other world religions since the 1960s has made us more aware of the force of Troeltsch's approach and of the need for humility amongst Christians in our dealings with people of other faiths lest we exacerbate division and fragmentation in our society. The explosion of new religions has demonstrated the extent to which traditional Christian faith and practice have lost their appeal for so many.

At the present time the historical relativity recognised by Troeltsch is receiving greater notice as modernity gives way to post-modernity. Evolution points us to the contingency of all things. It is claimed that there are no absolutes and no objective truth — and a good thing too because every claim to absoluteness is merely a disguised attempt to oppress and to compel conformity. Every world-view or meta-narrative is to be resisted as a weapon of oppression.

There is no transcendent reality. The world is all there is and there is no pattern or purpose to the world's life. The most striking fact about history is its unpredictability. We have arrived at Cupitt's 'universal meltdown'.

There are different ways of looking at this latest development. It is both a protest against Enlightenment values and the product of them. It is the ultimate humanism and the end of humanism. It means the end of the rigidities of modernity with all its vetoes on faith and metaphysics and the dawn of a new respectability for personal belief. It is also the privatising of all religion and truth. And where anything goes, nothing matters.

THE CHRISTIAN RESPONSE

Vivian Green's fear is that the churches will either retreat into obscurantism or dissolve into total assimilation. We must hope that we do neither. There may be a middle way but we shall have to make a massive intellectual effort to find it and it will take a long time. We shall need patience, stamina, imagination, courage and intellectual honesty.

Let us be clear. The decline of the church in Western society will not be arrested by tampering with our structures, polishing up our evangelistic techniques, smartening up our premises or warming up the welcome we offer at the church door. These things may all be necessary for other reasons but they do not address the profound crisis of faith with which the new millennium opens.

The fundamental task is a theological one. We must lose our fear of theology and become properly serious about it. In particular, we must commit ourselves to a discipline within the whole theological enterprise, which is as old as the church, and which is generally known as 'apologetics'. It is a word not always understood — and sometimes seriously misunderstood — in the church at large. It has nothing to do with apologising for the faith. Nor should it be seen, as it often has been, merely as the defence of the given tradition of faith. Rather, it is concerned with the examination and elucidation of the tradition of faith handed down to us and the exploration of the relation between that faith and contemporary thinking and experience. It rests upon the confidence that all truth derives from the Spirit of truth and that, therefore, to engage in fearless and rigorous conversation with people of all shades of opinion and faith may lead us deeper into God. It also recognises that our apprehension of truth is always relative, partial and provisional and stands in need of enlarging and refining.

Apologetics must always be critical both of the whole Christian tradition and of secular and religious thought, lest it fall into the error of idolatry by giving too permanent a status to words and images which can only be of temporary value. It must always be imaginative as it seeks to make connections between the tradition and today's thought, to discern the new insights God is giving us and to forge new metaphors and analogies by which to make sense of things. It must always be prophetic by daring to identify the presence of God in our world, knowing all the time that its judgements may prove to be mistaken and will need to be changed as circumstances change. God is never still.[7]

It must not too easily be assumed that the aim of finding a compelling faith for the Western world, with all its turbulent intellectual history, can be achieved. It is by no means clear whether or how Christianity can become the public truth which shapes our society and gives it moral cohesion and meaning. The search, therefore, must be genuinely open-ended. We must stand alongside people of all persuasions in genuine dialogue with a willingness to listen and even a readiness to change our own thinking where honesty requires it. All too often apologetics is compromised by the assumption that we know the end result before the enquiry begins. To adopt that approach is to reveal a profound lack of faith. We must let go and risk ourselves to the pursuit of truth wherever it leads.

That last sentence would, of course, immediately be seen by many as suspect. Post-modern doubts about human competence to discover truth have already been mentioned. But to surrender to those hesitations is to deny the possibility of any meaningful intellectual discourse beyond the merely analytical and to end in despair. By all means let us be sensitive to our limitations and relativity, but let us also retain confidence in the capacity of the human mind to make some kind of sense of our experience. The first apologetic task is to find some justification for the use of our minds.

Given that we can do that, a number of fundamental matters clamour for attention. Religious language has to be recognised as the provisional, conditioned, symbolic commodity that it is. No presentation of the Christian faith has ever been free from cultural conditioning. Biblical and credal presentations are no exceptions. To realise that may be an unsettling experience but it is also liberating. It points us to the fact that faith is dynamic. It is at least as much a pilgrimage and a search as it is a finding.

If this is God's world, we must expect to find the revelation of God in the whole of our experience and not just in parts of it. Theologians used to distinguish between general revelation and special or particular revelation. I am not sure that that distinction is any longer useful. It leads too easily into obscurantism and complacency. Bible and tradition claim to recognise moments of peculiar intensity in revelation but the claim can only be valid if those moments illuminate and give meaning to the whole of our experience. They cannot run counter to it. Apologetics must take seriously the givenness of life — the nature of humanity with its intelligence, inventiveness, self-reflection and spirituality; the vital importance for us of relationships; the fact of evil and suffering; the progress which, despite all assertions of randomness, does seem to be discernible in the evolutionary process and so on.

No apologetics can hope to have compelling power without a realistic understanding of providence. Deism with its image of God as the transcendent but ultimately uninvolved architect of the universe was long since found to be a barren faith. If we cannot, in some understandable though not necessarily traditional way, speak of the activity of God within the world, we cannot expect our message to appeal. In the end, however much this essay may appear to suggest otherwise, the Christian religion is not so much an intellectual exercise as a relationship with a living God and a way of living.

My own personal view is that all these challenges may be met by a theology resting upon a sufficiently radical understanding of the concept of grace. Grace in the sense of God's creative and positive letting-be allows for the possibility of an open creation. It explains the absence of any ultimate authority for truth or faith. The pale reflection of it which we sometimes manage in human relationships is what keeps the world turning. It leads us to expect a God who is hidden yet all-pervasive, self-limiting in action yet endlessly persuasive. It may even hold the key to the solution of the problem of suffering.

Of course, such notions may be naively romantic. Or they may be true. One millennium opportunity is to test them out with as much rigour, realism and integrity as we can muster.

NOTES

1. Sutton Publishing, 1996, p. 401.
2. *The Unacceptable Face*, (SCM, 1987), p. 220.
3. *After God* (Weidenfeld and Nicolson, 1997), p. 72.
4. Ibid., p. 75.
5. SCM, 1972, p. 46.
6. Ibid., p. 9.
7. Some of the material in this section was previously published in an article in the *Methodist Conference Handbook* (1997), p. 13.

QUESTIONS

1 What do you see as the greatest challenge to Christian faith?

2 Is a convergence of world faiths possible or desirable?

3 Where, if anywhere, do you find God?

4 What do you mean by grace? Does it offer any answer to today's questions?

A Young Person's Perspective

Catherine Wells

THE WORLD TODAY

It is easy as we look towards the next century to become depressed, to see the future as bleak, full of environmental disaster, bombing, war, dictators, genetic engineering and a decline of moral standards with which young Christians increasingly find themselves under pressure to conform. With hopefully many years of my life to come before me, I cannot help but wonder if the next millennium will see a disastrous dawn for the human race, in which normal human relations of family, marriage, love are destroyed by genetic cloning and moral relativity, the earth's beauty and resources are whittled away or even in which there could be a third and perhaps final world war. The young people I work with every day deal with issues and problems of divorced parents, drugs, alcohol, sexuality, violence and conflicting moral values. They establish their own protective armour; a don't care, sometimes aggressive attitude which warns others not to get too close. We are living in a world which is full of broken people, young and old, struggling through life and desperately searching for some truth or certainty. A world in which nothing is ever really wrong and few people are willing to accept blame for their own actions. Yet in this world, difficult as it is to believe at times, Jesus Christ is alive, still present and still real. He walks with the lonely and lost and reaches out to the struggling and suffering. God created this world and every person in it and there is far more beauty and hope around us than we allow ourselves to see.

We are living in God's world. His hand is over us, shaping our future and I firmly believe that, with God, the future can only be exciting. The future is not full of doom and gloom but of opportunities to serve the living Christ and reach out with his hands of love to the broken and confused people, young and old. Christ is the only answer to life, the universe and everything and we must be bold enough to share that glorious truth with others.

CHRIST IN OUR WORLD

I see the living Christ in situations where Christians are living and working to make a difference, where people raise their hands in worship and praise, or youngsters get excited about painting the church lounge in multi-colours, where church councils talk uncertainly but enthusiastically about reaching the community and sharing the love of God, where people reach out with Jesus' hands of love to welcome in the broken and the rejoicing alike.

It is all too easy to become depressed and down-hearted at the state of the world. We need to remember the reason for the millennium, which is God coming in person to save his people, for he loves the world, the whole world so much 'that he gave his only Son ... to be its saviour' (John 3:16–17). As a young Christian, I find it's important to remember this and I hold on to this powerful truth in a world which is constantly tempting me to fit in with everybody else. We are called as Christians to be in the world, not of it, and the challenge to the church today is to continue Christ's work in this world, good or bad as it is.

CHRIST'S CHURCH IN THE WORLD

Again, it's easy to look at the depressing side of life and bemoan the fact that membership is dropping and young people are abandoning the church in great numbers, but I want to emphasise the importance of finding God at work in the church, using ordinary people — you and me — to further his Kingdom. Over the last few years I have felt increasingly excited and privileged to be a young person in the Methodist Church. An odd thing to claim perhaps, but I have seen many inspiring things and hope to see many more into the next millennium.

Recently, I was one of a Seed Team of three people, working on a council estate in South Wales. It was hard and sometimes unrewarding but, throughout, the people of the church in that area held on to the vision that God had given them and worked towards it with a faithfulness which was inspiring. During the year we saw the worst and the best of God's world; his broken and hurting people but also the deep-rooted need they have for him. Most powerful of all was the way in which God used us ordinary people in his work. He took our gifts and talents, even our weaknesses, and used them in his service. I saw this again and saw the transforming power of God at work in a church when I took part in a Share Jesus mission in 1996. I've seen God at work in the Methodist Church, just in ordinary, local churches that have sought to serve God in whatever way they could.

In thinking about how God uses his people, the church in this broken world, I am reminded of a most moving incident at Easter People this year. A plea was made for assistance to be given to a church in Albania which was besieged by refugees flooding across the border from Kosovo. Over the course of two days, £25,000 was raised and the shops of Bournemouth were swept clean of shampoo, soap, toothpaste and sleeping bags to fill three lorries which were dispatched to Albania in a direct answer to the prayers of the workers in the church in Albania. There was such warm generosity on the part of the people at the event and I could feel God moving amongst us, using our resources to provide for others. It struck me that this is how our loving God, who hears the prayers and cries of his children, brings goodness and love into a situation which appears full of hatred and hopelessness. Again, God used the resources of his people to meet the needs of others suffering in the world.

CHALLENGES OF THE NEW MILLENNIUM

One of the most exciting challenges the Methodist Church faces is that of Charter '95; the vision for the church which arose from the work of young people across the country. It reveals that many young people are not about to give up and leave the church, but want to see it grow, change and meet the needs of all its members into the next millennium. This is something I sense strongly amongst many young people in Methodism; the willingness to fight hard and see the church change and move forward rather than stagnate and die. Charter '95 has been adopted by the Methodist Conference and its ideas are slowly disseminating amongst churches at local levels. It presents the vision of a church for the next century which is God centred, open and inclusive, challenges injustice, 'oozes its spirituality at every level' and provides 'radical, creative and relevant worship' for all. The challenge now is to pick up the ideas, capture the vision and start working prayerfully towards it, no matter who or where you are. It is a vision we can all own and commit ourselves to.

Charter '95 is a vision for the church into the next millennium, but it is not going to be easy. Each individual church needs not just to OK it, but to take it on board and collectively accept it as what we will work and strive for in our own church and community. No small task, but a challenge we can rise to.

CONCLUDING THOUGHTS

As we go into the next thousand years let's face up to the weaknesses but also the enormous strengths of the church. Ask how we can carry out the commission with which Jesus left us; to go 'to all peoples everywhere and make them [his] disciples'. It is the job of the church to continue Christ's work. It is not an optional extra but a command which demands sacrifice and commitment 100% of the time. Jesus never promised an easy ride, a cosy church to come to in order to escape from life. He demanded and still does that his followers should put themselves on the line, stand up for what is right and respond to the needs of the hurting people around them, in the power of his love. He, in return, promises always to be with us, giving guidance and providing the gifts and love we need to carry out his work.

With him we can rise to the challenges of the next century, taking up the vision the church has already accepted in Charter '95. We can build on the strengths we have and commit our individual gifts, no matter what our age and ability, to God's service.

QUESTIONS

1 Where can you see God at work in the world and in the Church?

2 How do you feel about the vision of Charter '95? Can you accept it? What can you do about it?

3 What gifts do you have which you can commit to God?

ABOUT CHARTER '95

Part One consists of a vision for the church:

- Our church must be a place where God is central to everything;
- The Bible and prayer are considered crucial;
- The focus of decision and action is on God's will;
- The way of Jesus is examined and closely followed;
- There is an expectation that, through the Holy Spirit, lives will be touched and change will take place.

1 Open and inclusive: realise that opinions will differ in our church.
(a) Encourage a culture of dialogue in which all can be honest and open about what they believe.
(b) Address issues of racism, sexism, ageism ... and other forms of prejudice in and outside the church.

2 Power imbalances addressed: recognise that power operates in subtle ways. Decision-making processes can benefit one group more than another.
(a) Address in particular issues relating to lay and ordained, adult and youth and all the 'isms'.
(b) Provide support for those with less power when they feel it necessary to tackle authority.

3 Radical, creative and relevant worship: balancing the best of old and new.
(a) Develop the use of audio, video, drama, local gifts and the full range of musical possibilities open to the congregation.
(b) Make the message relevant. The style should be suitable and influenced by the needs of a generation that has no church background.

4 High profile action: to be as much a part of church life as the Sunday Service.
(a) Challenge injustice, prejudice, be active in the community, tackle issues of concern.
(b) Look at creative ways of involving new people.

5 Facilities suitable for a modern church: recognise the importance of image and atmosphere of premises.
(a) Aim to include modern facilities (e.g. technology, musical equipment) in a relaxed environment.

Part Two contains practical suggestions on how to achieve the aims above, for example:

- Promote new ideas and group work methods to make meetings more interesting and creative;
- Look for ways of reducing the committee workload on church members;
- Devise a brave new programme to develop worship, e.g. use of worship leaders, training extended to refresher courses (e.g. for all age worship), wider range of musical instruments;
- Ensure committees do not become dominated by members of a particular tradition.

Dare we face the challenge?

Doctrine: Death to the Spirit or Life?

Georgina Morley

> There is one physician, fleshly and spiritual, begotten and unbegotten, God in man, true life in death, both of Mary and of God, first passible then impassible, Jesus Christ our Lord.
> Ignatius AD 112

> This is the faith that we hold from beginning to end, and before God and Christ. Therefore we anathematise every heretical false opinion.
> Athanasius AD 341

DIFFICULTIES WITH DOCTRINE

DURING its 2,000 years the Church has accumulated a vast amount of *doctrine*: official beliefs and traditional formulae for expressing the faith, for explaining about Jesus as God and man, for talking about God as Trinity, for thinking about the beginning and the end of everything. Whether we recognise it or not, all our believing is shaped by this communal teaching. All our praying and reading the Bible is influenced by the Church's doctrinal tradition.

Although these doctrines have all been developed from the best of motives, from reflection on Scripture and an attempt to be faithful to who God seems to reveal himself to be, they are also shaped by the time and culture in which they appear. This gives them a certain ambiguity. On the one hand, they are often expressed in difficult and archaic language and in ideas that can seem irrelevant, or repellent, or at worst morally offensive to us. On the other hand, they tweak some instinct in us which is trying to hold us open to God — to know God, to hear God, to grow in God. Along with mysterious and difficult passages in the Bible they invite us to *believe*, to cast ourselves recklessly into something a little bit bigger than reason and common sense offer, in the hopeful trust that God is calling us to be and believe always *more*. Doctrine can be archaic ... and yet alluring. It can be alienating ... but also inviting.

This ambiguity which comes from the nature of doctrine itself is something which Christians have always had to face. But now we have an additional problem: we are living in a culture which is suspicious of authority — of other people telling us what we should do and think and believe. We are wary of other people trying to impress their truth claims on us: 'Why should we think that this is a genuine insight into what is *true*? It might be an attempt to control us, to limit our choices, to lure us from our better judgement. We must work out our *own* truth, find our *own* way, select the belief and practices which suit our *own* personality...'. In this climate sometimes the Church simply follows the culture and makes no truth claims, plays down the teaching it has inherited from its faithful forebears and merely lays out a range of spiritual 'merchandise' to choose from. The danger is of the cheap grace that Dietrich Bonhoeffer warns of: 'Cheap grace is the grace we bestow on ourselves. It is the preaching of forgiveness without requiring repentance, baptism without discipline, communion without confession. Cheap grace is grace without discipleship, grace without the cross, grace without Jesus Christ living and incarnate.'[1] Sometimes, however, the Church reacts too strongly the other way and becomes too dogmatic, too insistent, too defensive of its claim to the truth. The faithful are spoon-fed and there is none of that risky launching out into God's unknown which must characterise those of us who follow in the footsteps of Abraham and Moses, Mary and the apostles, Bonhoeffer himself.

So then, if doctrine is tricky, it is trickier still at the turn of the millennium. Can it be rescued, wrestled away from a suspicious culture or a dogmatic minority, from archaic and unfortunate language? Can it be a resource for our faith into the next millennium? Yes; wholeheartedly *yes* — so long as we don't insist on its irrelevance, but understand that we have a part to play in its continuing life and development.

HOW DOCTRINE HAPPENS

The first and most important thing is to note how doctrines come about. Certainly it is the case that when theologians in the Church pay attention to a reality and truth revealed by God, a precisely formulated statement is always the result: 'truly God and truly man', for example. This formula marks some boundaries against error and misunderstanding and allows for clarity and security. But it is not intended to be an end in itself, fossilised and passed on intact through the generations. It is meant to be a *beginning* — a beginning to reflection and thinking, to help future generations press on more deeply into the truth it sketchily records. This 'pressing on' is the task of *everyone* in the church, so that the doctrine stays alive, better understood, better lived, better expressed in each age and place. This means that doctrine is *not* about dry, static formulae of right thinking that we simply have to agree to. A 'doctrine' is not a single coherent theory. It's not something that has been carefully worked out in the past, something that has already happened, which we just inherit ready made. It is something 'on the way', which we participate in.

Doing doctrine is about *us* being part of the community (past and present) who have been faced with this extraordinary thing of God's gift of himself in Jesus Christ and who have had to think what to make of that, how to understand it, how to live in the light of it, how to go on making sense of it no matter how things change in the world, how to go on expressing it so that it is clear and relevant to that time and situation and how to go on being open to the revelation — to be challenged and comforted and renewed by it. *Doctrine is about living as a member of a community; it's about fully inhabiting the community of faith to which we belong, and appropriating its beliefs for ourselves. Doctrine is about living as part of a community that knows God and longs for God.*

So doctrine is about being open to what is *most true*, and about keeping on pointing to God and to what God has shown us of himself. Doctrine is how the Church keeps a faithful sense of the *present reality* of God's promises. And how it keeps on asking, 'What does it mean for *us* to be the Church, to be Christians? How shall *we* keep the faith?' Doctrine is the connection between God's revelation of himself in Jesus and the New Testament's witness to that, and the living Church in every age which is keeping faithful to that revelation.

The doctrines that we have, the teachings and the formulae, the stuff that feels quite static, is simply the accumulation of other people doing that; it's the markers of other people's faithfulness to what we're trying to be faithful to.

It's not a collection of right answers, but markers, signposts that say, 'the path is here, if you go that way you step off the path, but over here seems to be the right direction'.

The authority it has lies in the initiative of God and the experience of God, not in a logical right answer or the power of the Church Fathers over us. It is the authority of the community being faithful to God — which means being renewed by God and being judged by God, as well as just talking about God. It has authority both because we place some confidence in the faith and discernment of those who have known God before us and because it refers to something beyond itself that's true — to the activity of God in this community and in our world. That's actually a much more passionate and compelling and *inviting* authority.

There is a very helpful picture which shows what this means in practice:

BROWSING IN THE FILES

Imagine a very battered filing cabinet, full to bursting point with files. The files themselves are overflowing and dog-eared, obviously in constant use. And they are very disorganised; it's hard to tell if they are in any order at all. If you open a file, you will find a certain amount of chaos. There will be a few neatly typed documents — formal reports and summaries, obviously written at various different times, and masses of scraps of paper, backs of old envelopes, handwritten tirades and heated replies, lists, the odd sermon ... a filing cabinet to drive the church administrator *crazy*!

The Church's whole doctrinal system is like this filing cabinet. Each file represents one doctrine, so they're labelled Trinity, Incarnation, Creation and so on. The neat documents are the statements the church makes from time to time when it thinks it has arrived at some definitive understanding, or wants to clarify things by saying, 'This is what we think about the resurrection at the moment'. So there may be something from AD 325, the Council of Nicaea, when the Church decided on the expression 'truly God and truly man', or the recent report from the Church of England *The Mystery of Salvation*. The scraps of paper are all the other bits of thinking and insight that happen along the way. Some of them will appear to contradict one another, but they all more or less point in the same direction, to the same broad truth. Some of them seem pretty archaic and irrelevant, though they may have been a helpful basis for something later on; some will seem pretty exciting. Some will be absolutely crucial; some will be interesting but marginal. No one thing in the file will tell you the whole story — you couldn't pick one thing out and say 'ah, now I understand the Trinity'. And the whole file is rather confusing, but really quite accurate. And although it's all a bit of a nightmare you know that, like stepping through the wardrobe to Narnia, it's very important and significant — that somehow it tells you who you are and where you belong and what your destiny is. It points you forward to a larger truth that you can't quite grasp yet. It doesn't matter that you haven't got the hang of it all, as long as you're delving in.

That's the state of doctrine in the Church. When you want to think about the Trinity, say, it's like pulling out one of those files and immersing yourself in it. You don't have to read through it all at once systematically, but every little helps to orientate you and to immerse you in the community of those who are following Christ.

A COLOUR FILTER ON THE WORLD

Another picture will help to explain how doctrines *work* and why they are helpful for the way we live and believe in the world. Imagine a selection of different colour filters and how different things look when you look at the world through the various colours. Everything is sort of the same but sort of different. Some things are enhanced, even exaggerated, and some things almost disappear. And depending which colour you're looking through, it is different things which become clearer or more difficult to see.

The different colour filters are different doctrines and when you look at the world through a different doctrine things are 'coloured' very differently. So, for example, if you have a cross-centred faith, and look at the world through the cross-coloured filter, what stands out very clearly is that things in the world have fallen short of what God intends and that God has acted decisively and at cost to sort things out. This is a world-transforming faith and to join in God's work is to recognise what needs transformation and to act with him. On the other hand, if you have a creation-centred faith, a creation-coloured filter, you will see how God delights in the world, how close it is to him, how it pleases him. It is a world-affirming faith and you will share in God's work by affirming what is good and holy wherever it is found. Both ways of seeing the world are true but neither is wholly true alone.

If we are growing more deeply into God's truth, this way of understanding the effect of doctrines can be very helpful. We each have a bias, a favourite filter, a doctrinal preference, just like we all have a bit of the Bible that we find especially fruitful. It's fine to have a bias, because it gives us strengths to play to. But it's valuable to look through a different filter from time to time — to make sure our faith is balanced, to look at the bits we don't see with our usual filter, to restore balance to things which our usual filter exaggerates. In short, to make sure we're living the *whole* faith. Just as if you met someone who had only ever read one part of the Bible — the book of Job, for example, you'd want to say to them, 'Well, what you see isn't wrong, what you have found out about God isn't wrong. But read a gospel and see what you discover then!'

GIVING IT A GO

When we read a passage from the Bible, probably even without thinking about it we go through several stages. We notice what the *point* of the piece is (for example, Jesus told the story of the Good Samaritan *to make the point that...*); we look to see where we *encounter* it in our own experience (who is a Good Samaritan *in our world*?); we ask ourselves how we can *live* more truly to what the passage calls us to (who should *I* be a Good Samaritan to?); and we *pray* the passage ('Help me to recognise who my neighbour is and to be generous to meet their need'). To understand and live a doctrine we can do exactly the same thing. This means we must:

- *Explore* the doctrine: what is the *point* of this teaching — what has the community of faith tried to express about its experience of God in this teaching?
- *Encounter* the doctrine: where do I see this in my experience in the world?

- *Live* the doctrine: how can I live in the truth of this teaching, what difference will believing this make to the way I am in the world?
- *Pray* the doctrine: if I believe this, how will it shape and inform my praying?

So, have a go. Choose a doctrine, a colour filter; something that already colours the way you look at the world, or something that is unfamiliar to you, through which you would like to see how the world looks. (If you don't know where to begin, start with the doctrine of the Incarnation: in Jesus Christ God has lived a human life in the world.) And work through these four ways into the doctrine. Take plenty of time to reflect and discuss each one. *Dare to live* the faith that the Christians who have already followed Christ before us have lived and to make it a reality to those who live with us at the turn of the millennium and to keep it alive for the people who will follow us.

NOTE

1. Dietrich Bonhoeffer, *The Cost of Discipleship* (ET London: SCM, 1959), p. 36.

A Theology of Good Intentions

Anthony Reddie

This essay has its roots deeply embedded within the doctoral research I have been undertaking on behalf of the 'Birmingham Initiative'[1], working alongside Black Christians in inner-city churches in Birmingham. These reflections are very much a work 'in progress', and will be subject to refinements and amendments at a later point, most probably in the later chapters of my doctoral thesis and any subsequent publications. At this juncture, it is offered as a nascent theory that is attempting to delineate aspects of the ongoing experiences and realities of Black people worshipping within Methodism.

I commence this piece by introducing a training exercise and the accompanying reflections, as a means of explicating the phenomenological framework that gave rise to this hypothesis.[2] This exercise provides not only a useful introduction, but it will, I hope, enable the reader to conceptualise the nature and effect of what I have termed, 'A Theology of Good Intentions'.

WHO IS INVITED TO THE PARTY?

A training exercise: action

- Assemble the group into two halves. Ask one half of the group to walk to the right side of the room and the other group to walk to the left.
- Inform both groups that you will be holding a party on the first Friday of each month. As the one who has ultimate power and authority, you are in a position to decide who will be coming to your party.
- You inform the group on the right that they will be invited to the party. Every Friday they will be asked to attend your party.
- You inform the group on the left that they will never be invited to your party. They must never set foot in your place on a Friday.
- Inform both groups that a week has gone by. You had the party on the Friday, but you forgot to invite the group on the right to your party on the Friday as you had promised. You fully intended to, but you simply forgot. How do they feel hearing this news?
- Inform the group on the left that they were never invited to the party. It is too bad for them.

- Having apologised to the group on the right and promised them that they will be invited to the next party, you remind the group on the left that they will never be invited.
- You inform both groups that another week has past and that you forgot to invite the group on the right once again. You fully intended to, but once again, you forgot. How do they feel, having been promised, but then overlooked when the party took place? How does the group on the left feel, having not been invited at all?
- Repeat the above operation on another five or six occasions. How does the group on the right feel? What about the group on the left? Does the group on the right feel at an advantage, having been informed that they were invited to (even though they have never attended) the party?

REFLECTION ON THE EXERCISE

The above exercise is intended to represent the Church's attempt to be inclusive in its treatment of black and minority ethnic people within the faith community. In a great number of instances, black people are denied full access to the whole life of the church, in terms of holding office, being in positions of authority where the decisions are being made, feeling fully at home in the church, etc.[3]. The two groups represent differing attitudes to black people by the church, particularly, those who hold office and exercise power and authority in the church.

The group on the left represents the old attitude. One that was uncompromising in its view of black people. Quite simply black people were not welcome and were certainly not invited to be a part of the church. This was the attitude that faced many black people when a majority of them first came to Britain in the 1950s and 60s. Not only were they not welcomed, on many occasions, they were told explicitly to leave the church. This attitude was very hurtful. Many of the black majority churches in Britain developed from this outright rejection from the 'main-line' churches.

The group on the right represents a more contemporary attitude — the attitude that prevails today. This is the attitude of good intentions. It is one that always attempts to do the right thing. It is the attitude that has its heart in the right place. Yet, as we saw from the exercise, it does not get any further than mere rhetoric. The people to whom the promise is made never find themselves at the party on the Friday. In many respects their plight is even worse than the group on the right, because they have been made promises that the host of the party has never kept. Whether the host accidentally forgot, or whether it was a conscious decision, is largely irrelevant, because, either way, these people still find themselves outside of the party. For the people on the left to whom no promise was ever made, they have nothing to expect, so they are less disappointed than those in the group on the right.

Eventually, over a period of time, the group on the right will become tired of hearing the seemingly hollow promises of the host. They will most likely refuse to listen to the hollow words and will decide for themselves that they do not want to attend the party at all, even if a later invite was a genuine one. It is the case that for some black people they have grown tired of the many promises made by the church and have decided that they are no longer interested in being included in the central heart of the church. They have been let down too often to take the rhetoric seriously anymore.

The church, in all its decision-making and ways of operating, must attempt to move away from a culture and a theology of good intentions, and must find ways of delivering on the high promises and fine words that have been spoken for too many years now. The church must have strategies and policies that can be implemented, and monitoring should be in order to ensure that those promises are being put into effect and are seen to be working. If not, then the fine words and promises will remain just that, and black people will continue to find themselves elsewhere when the party is taking place, despite the warm promises and many kind words.

ANALYSIS AND REFLECTION

The above exercise and accompanying reflections have been shared with a number of lay and ordained folk in inner-city Methodist churches in Birmingham for several months. The exercise has found full accord with the many black people who have taken part in this training exercise. The metaphor of the party was a useful conceit, for it typifies to a great effect the pain and frustration felt by those who are marginalised.

From what source does this theology of good intentions originate? I believe there are two sources for this paternalistic and patrician attitude that is often manifested in the life of the church. First and foremost, it owes much to our perception of Jesus as depicted in the Gospels. As James Cone reminds us, 'Christian theology begins and ends with Jesus Christ'.[4] The Jesus we identify with is the 'Gentle Jesus meek and mild' of our childhood prayers and Christian education and nurture in Sunday school. It is a Jesus 'Who never said a mumbling word' in the face of his detractors. It is a view of Jesus where the overturning of the tables in the temple is either a temporary aberration or can be explained away in pious terms with the well-worn phrase of 'righteous anger'. Not ordinary anger, you understand, but anger that is essentially moral and blameless.

A 'Theology of Good Intentions' is predicated upon the notion that 'sorry' is the response to issues of injustice and marginalisation. It matters less that the conditions that give rise to such oppression and marginalisation are often untouched or remain unchallenged. Systemic abuses and institutionalised racism continue to flourish, as they are often disguised with the all-embracing veneer of apologetic rhetoric.

This 'Theology of Good Intentions' becomes all the more pernicious for the effects it has upon the recipient. Think back to the exercise a moment. On a number of occasions when this has been enacted, those playing[5] the host have become indignant at the refusal of invitees who have been continually shunned, to acknowledge the good faith of the one who is issuing the invite. The individuals who refuse to accept the continuing apologies of the host are deemed to be people who have 'chips on their shoulders', or possess 'attitude problems'. On occasions, the words of a passive and supine Jesus are liberally introduced into the proceedings, reminding the recalcitrant malcontent that we are to 'turn the other cheek' and 'forgive seventy times seven'.

Forgiveness in response to the ubiquitous 'sorry' is the order of the day, but little if anything is said concerning justice and repentance. Once the word 'sorry' is invoked, it is expected to suffice with no concomitant cognisance of the incident or situation until the next apology is issued, often, for the same oversight that was committed previously. Failure to forgive, or to collude in this unhealthy and unhelpful scenario is to earn the disapprobation of those who commit the offence in the first instance. One is condemned for being 'unchristian'. I have heard the words, 'Now would Jesus have done that?' used to validate the actions of the host and their continual recourse to the mechanism of the apologetic. The apology is surgically removed from the injustice and systemic inequalities that rendered the apology necessary.

In order to put this nascent theory into some form of context, let me share a story with you. The details are not necessary, and I need not identify any of the major players, as it is not my intention to cause undue embarrassment or hurt. At the 1998 Methodist Conference in Scarborough, an unfortunate *faux pas* was committed from the platform at the end of a very poignant and painful Notice of Motion on the experiences of black people in Britain, in the Methodist church and the wider society. The debate was concerned with institutionalised racism in the church.

I am absolutely convinced that the unfortunate words were not intended to cause offence, and the resulting apology was heartfelt and sincere. Yet, what concerned me was the number of people who approached me and other black colleagues at Conference saying 'how unfortunate it all was' and 'what an honest mistake it had been'. In reply to one such individual I said, 'So that makes it alright now?' He did not have an answer for my question. The apology, you see, was sufficient. Despite the poignancy of the debate, the open wounds that were being expressed by a number of bruised and pained older black people, many of whom had been at the forefront of an ongoing negation (much like those in the exercise to whom invites had been made but never delivered), it was still felt that a little levity was appropriate for such an occasion.

Let me remind you that this incident took place in 1998, not 1958, or 1978. In one respect, we can view this as nothing more than an unfortunate mistake. Yet, I feel it is symptomatic of an organisation that has not moved beyond the rhetoric of apology. I am not aware of any analysis or investigation into how or why this incident should have happened. After all, had the debate been concerned with child abuse, violence or sexual harassment, I doubt the need for humour would have been deemed appropriate.

One may assume that despite the heartfelt entreaties of those black speakers, their experiences of exclusion or marginalisation from the party were not heard sufficiently, or even more frighteningly, were not taken seriously.

A 'Theology of Good Intentions' is predicated on a passive, forgiving notion of God. A God who will not condemn or call to account. It is time we began to move beyond the rhetoric and began to analyse why things are the way they are. Why is the church in its official functioning and representative life so far removed from the reality and diversity of the whole church? Why is it still the case that in a church that is irrefutably multi-cultural, the image one receives of the corporate church is steadfastly white and middle-class? Mere good intentions and warm platitudes will not correct this distortion. Prayerful action and real repentance are but the start.

NOTES

1. The 'Birmingham Initiative', a Methodist-inspired ecumenical research project that is attempting to develop a theory and an accompanying methodology for the Christian education of black children and young people. The project has worked collaboratively with 26 churches from the Methodist, Baptist, Anglican and URC traditions. All the churches are situated within the inner-city areas of Birmingham. The membership of these churches is predominantly black, African Caribbean. I am greatly indebted to many of these black lay people (particularly the children) for their co-operation and assistance in the development of this theory.
2. This exercise was developed as a part of the empirical research within the 'Birmingham Initiative'. Its development reflected my attempts as the researcher to operate within an action-reflection paradigm — one in which the researcher acknowledges their reflexivity within the research, and attempts to act in a dialogical and collaborative fashion with his other co-researchers. This training exercise was an attempt to explicate an important theme that had emerged in the course of the empirical work and had been detected and

reflected upon by myself. I wanted to find an accessible means of sharing this emergent theme with the significant others in the research project.

3 See volume two of my book, *Growing into Hope*, Vol. 2, *Liberation and Change* (Methodist Publishing House, Peterborough, 1998), pp. 8-10.

4 James H. Cone, *A Black Theology of Liberation* (Maryknoll, New York: Orbis Books, 1970), p. 110.

5 In the enactment of these exercises, individuals are encouraged to get into character and be as realistic in their portrayal as possible. Whilst the exercise is an educational conceit, and whilst it is clearly the case that participants can and do 'pretend' to play along with the role assigned them, nevertheless, it is hoped that individuals will attempt to enter into the internal logic of the exercise on its own terms.

QUESTIONS

1 Have there been any occasions/situations when you have experienced a form of marginalisation that might be linked to the exercise I described in the essay? How did you feel? Is that situation still in evidence?

2 How can the (Methodist) Church move beyond fine words and good intentions?

3 What is your understanding of an 'inclusive' and 'open' church?

4 What is your vision for an inclusive and open church? How could that come about?

An Ecumenical Vision

Stuart J. Burgess

PENTECOST SUNDAY 2000 is being celebrated as an ecumenical occasion throughout the country. In large regional areas and small village communities plans are being made for Christians to gather from all denominations for a millennium celebration. Village halls, community centres, parks and stadiums are now booked for Christians to gather and celebrate the birth of Christ 2,000 years ago. All these festivities beg the question, 'To what end and for what purpose?' Is this a one-off occasion or are the churches sending a signal to society that Christian people are committed to seek unity amongst themselves and witness together in the world? My hope is for the latter.

The 20th century has been one in which great strides have been made ecumenically. Of course there will be those who will be frustrated by the lack of pace, but as we now reflect over the last 100 years it is important to recognise that a good deal of prejudice has disappeared. Christians, on the whole, are more tolerant of each other and competition is giving way to co-operation. There is a long way to go but it may be concluded that the ecumenical events of the 20th century have paved the way for important breakthroughs in the 21st century. churches have been divided for centuries and there is no such thing as cheap reconciliation, as the cross demonstrates.

Since the 1950s the ecumenical movement has developed quickly and this may partly be due to the Second World War providing a watershed within society and the Church. It is certainly true that society has not been the same since and as changes in society affect the life of the Church (i.e. the role of women) then the churches have to respond to change.

There are many building blocks which can be identified in the 20th century which give rise for hope in the future. Of course, there were failures such as the Anglican/Methodist scheme in the 1960s and the Covenant Proposals of the 1970s. Yet out of apparent failure came the growth of eucharistic hospitality between Anglicans and Methodists and later the establishment of Local Ecumenical Projects (now Partnerships). Vatican II was a significant milestone, not only in the Roman Catholic Church, but throughout Christendom. There now seems to be a greater openness especially between Roman Catholics and Protestants.

Two reports — 'Faith in the City' and 'Faith in the Countryside' — Anglican initiatives with ecumenical input, highlighted the sociological and social issues of the 1980s and posed important questions for the churches. The Church was called to face realities such as the multi-faith context, living in a post-industrial society and the continuing drift from the countryside to the town.

The British Council of churches came to an end and flowered into Churches Together in Britain and Ireland, and Churches Together in England. These ecumenical instruments are still discovering their role in the national scene but bring together a wide range of different church allegiance. It is a joy that the Roman Catholic Church is fully involved. The publication of *Called to be One* by Churches Together in England is a useful resource book concerning the visible unity of the Church.

The growth industry in unity has come from local initiatives and through the establishment of Local Ecumenical Partnerships (LEPs). There are four hundred and forty five LEPs between Anglican and Methodist Churches. In other words local churches and groups of Christians have often set the pace and found their way through the red tape of constitutions and worked out for themselves what it means to be the Church in a particular area. All credit to them. Some have failed but many have flourished and continue to grow. At their best LEPs recognise each other's ministry, share the riches of their spirituality and work together for the sake of the community. Examples of good practice are numerous and tribute should be paid to clergy and laity who are determined to be the visible Church in the area. Heslington, near York, is one of the oldest LEPs in the country having recently celebrated its silver jubilee. It responded to the needs of the village churches, Anglican and Methodist, and to the huge development of the establishment of the University of York.

Other examples include LEPs being established in villages, new housing estates and inner cities. In very profound ways LEPs have given an impetus to the ecumenical movement.

Other important building blocks may be identified, such as:

Ut Unum Sint — the encyclical letter of the Holy Father, John Paul II on commitment to ecumenism. John Paul writes: 'ecumenism, the movement promoting Christian unity, is not just some sort of appendix which is added to the Church's traditional activity. Rather, ecumenism is an organic part of her life and work and consequently must pervade all that she is, and does.' (Para 20, p. 26, *Ut Unum Sint*).

Sharing in the Apostolic Communion is the Report of the Anglican-Methodist International Commission to the World Methodist Council and the Lambeth Conference. It encourages Anglicans and Methodists to grow together in worship, mutual care and mission together. The report also points us forward in terms of: mutual recognition of members, mutual recognition and interchangeability of ministries and rites and structures of common decision-making.

The Anglican-Moravian Conversations concerned the conversations between the Church of England and the Moravian Church in Great Britain and Ireland, which is among the Church of England's oldest ecumenical partners. The Fetter Lane Common Statement sets out the extensive agreement between these two historic episcopal churches. It also makes recommendations of immediate practical steps towards visible unity.

The Porvoo Common Statement is the report on the conversations between the British and Irish Anglican Churches and the Nordic and Baltic Lutheran Churches.

It sets out to resolve long-standing difficulties about episcopal succession, opening the way to a reconciled common ministry. Its acceptance by the churches involved means that the Porvoo Common Statement can be a building block for the future.

An interesting idea has come from Wales with the report 'Toward the making of an Ecumenical Bishop in Wales'. The Covenanted Churches in Wales believe that they should mark the advent of the millennium by consecrating an Ecumenical Bishop in Wales 'who shall be in full communion with us as with all other churches party to the scheme'. The area has been defined as Cardiff East and beyond, including Cyncoed, Pentwyn, Llanedeym and St Mellon's and builds upon Local Ecumenical Partnerships. A brave venture which deserves to succeed.

By far the most important report, as we celebrate the millennium, is *Commitment to Mission and Unity*. This is the report of the Informal Conversations between the Methodist Church and the Church of England. The idea began in the autumn of 1993 with an approach from the Methodist Church to the Church of England to begin informal talks to see if it was worthwhile beginning Formal Conversations. The report was discussed and voted upon at the Gereral Synod of the Church of England in November 1997 and at the Methodist Conference in June 1998. Both bodies overwhelmingly supported the recommendations:

- To encourage our Churches to grow together in fellowship
- To initiate Formal Conversations between our Churches and to draw up a common statement which should include: a description of visible unity, an exploration of outstanding issues of difference and a declaration of acknowledgments and commitments.

All these 'building blocks' and many others have a number of common threads — such as the need for unity, exploration of the outstanding differences and a commitment to be the Church in the world for the sake of the gospel.

However, before we get carried away into some state of euphoria two basic questions need to be asked.

Why is there a need for unity amongst the churches? The theological basis for unity is in the Incarnation which is the visible embodiment of the Word of God in human nature (John 1:14). 'The Ministry, death and resurrection of Jesus and the gift of the Holy Spirit demonstrates the unity of God's being and God's desire that all creation should be drawn into that unity. These mighty acts of God require that the Church's unity should itself be visible' (*Commitment to Mission and Unity*, para 8, p. 5). The doctrine of the Trinity is the effective instrument of God's reconciling purpose and the authentic foretaste of the bringing of all things into a unity in Christ at the end of time.

The Church does not exist for itself but for the world. The mission of the Church is important and the work towards unity only gains importance when the Church seeks to be 'the people of God ' in that place.

As we enter the 3rd millennium all the churches face decline and limited resources in terms of money and person power. It makes economic and strategic sense to work together and pool our resources for the sake of the gospel. Certainly in villages, new housing developments, inner-city areas, there is no other way forward. The Church in rural areas — and this is in the main the Church of England and the Methodist Church — has about 10 years to re-think its common strategies otherwise whole areas of the countryside will have no visible worshipping church community.

WHAT SORT OF UNITY DO WE SEEK?

We seek not organic unity, but a visibly united Church which would include the following important characteristics: a common profession of the one apostolic faith grounded in Holy Scriptures and set forth in the historic creeds; the sharing of one baptism and the celebrating of one eucharist; a common ministry of word and sacrament and a common ministry of oversight (episcope). (*Commitment to Mission and Unity*, para 10, p. 6).

Naturally, visible unity should not be confused with uniformity. All our churches are now quite diverse. Diversity is a strength but there may be limits to diversity if communion is to be maintained.

THE WAY AHEAD

The Roman Catholic Church is perhaps the unknown quantity in the new millennium. The present Holy Father is committed to ecumenism — perhaps on his terms — but the next Pope could set a new tone, break down barriers and offer a breakthrough in terms of Roman/Protestant relationships. Certainly Liberation Theology in Latin America and the younger

African churches are challenging many of the old structures. However, all this can only be speculation and we can only work with the opportunities that are now before us.

In England, *Commitment to Mission and Unity* provides us with a possible breakthrough between an Episcopal and non-Episcopal Church around which others may be able to gather, especially the United Reformed Church. The report identifies ten major issues to be resolved between the Church of England and the Methodist Church. These are listed below:

- **Initiation and Membership.** Methodism at present has a membership system and the Church of England an electoral roll system. Also, Confirmation in the Methodist Church is practised by local presbyters and in the Church of England only bishops can confirm.
- **Authorisation of lay persons to preside at the Eucharist.** In the Methodist Church probationer Ministers (who are not ordained) are normally authorised to preside. Other lay people may preside and the authorisations are granted by the Conference. The Church of England's position does not allow for lay presidency.
- **The threefold Ministry.** The Methodist Church recognises two orders of Ministry — presbyteral and diaconal. The Church of England has the threefold order of Ministry — bishop, presbyter and deacon.
- **The nature and role of the diaconate.** The Church of England does have some permanent deacons but regards diaconal orders as a prerequisite to the presbyterate. The Methodist Church has a permanent diaconate and presbyters are ordained directly.
- **The nature and style of the office of bishop.** The Church of England exercises oversight through bishops who are now often described as 'Bishop in Synod', stressing a collaborative style. The Methodist Church in England does not have bishops and exercises oversight through the President, Chairman of District and Circuit Superintendents.
- **The ordination of women to the episcopate.** In the Methodist Church women are able to hold any office in the Church. In the Church of England the legislation which allows women to be ordained as priests specifically excludes them from being consecrated bishops.
- **Reconciliation of ordained Ministries.** This may well be a 'hard nut' to crack but there are some interesting models, especially the model in *Facing Unity*, the report of the Roman Catholic-Lutheran Joint Commission. This report proposes a pattern of gradual reconciliation of ministries involving the setting up of preliminary forms of the joint exer-

cise of episcope, an initial act of recognition and the establishment of a single episcope in collegial form leading to a period of transition from the joint exercise of episcope to a common ordained ministry.

The other issues may be baldly stated:

- Structures of authority, oversight and government.
- The relation of Church and State.
- Relations to our world communions.

Arising from the above, the following call for comment:

Firstly, the Methodist Church must grasp the nettle concerning the threefold Ministry. The two orders of Ministry — the Presbyteral and Diaconal — is illogical and must be addressed. The history of the Church has formed its unity around the threefold order and it is inconceivable that an Episcopal Church will ever move away from this position. 'Bishop' is not foreign to World Methodism and many of the autonomous Conferences use the title bishop. Of course there is a reluctance in some quarters of Methodism to use the title and this is usually due to the images it brings to mind, e.g. power, status and palaces. Yet this is to deny the Methodist Church the responsibility of working out for itself the nature and office of bishop. The threefold order is looked upon as a gift of unity from the Episcopal Church and Methodism should embrace it at the earliest opportunity. With this acceptance then further theological work can be done around the three orders set within an ecumenical context.

Secondly, the Church of England must at some time in the next decade address the issue of the consecration of women as bishops. It is true that the legislation of the General Synod was a compromise to help keep the Church together — known by some as the 'Habgood solution' (Rt Revd John Habgood, former Archbishop of York). However, it can only be seen as an interim solution and there will be many women priests who in the next 20 years will make excellent bishops. It is important to note that a number of Provinces in the Anglican Communion have women bishops.

It is my hope that the Doctrine of Reception will in the first quarter of the next century accept the equal status of women and men in all aspects of the Church.

Thirdly, the historic Episcopate. A great deal has been written on this subject and many Methodists would be reluctant to accept the Apostolic succession in terms of the tactile act. Yet there are useful insights to be gleaned from *Sharing in the Apostolic Communion* and the *Porvoo Report* which states that 'To ordain a bishop in historic succession is a *sign* of the continuity, unity and catholicity of the Church' (para 50, p. 27).

The *Porvoo Report* also says,

> This means that those Churches in which the sign has at some time not been used are free to recognise the value of the sign and should embrace it without denying their own apostolic continuity. This also means that those Churches in which the sign has been used are free to recognise the reality of the Episcopal office and should affirm the apostolic continuity of those Churches in which the sign of Episcopal succession has at some time not been used.

It now seems that the formal conversations between the Church of England and Methodist Church could use the *Porvoo Report* as a basis for further reflection.

I believe that the main impetus for closer relations between the Church of England and the Methodist Church will come as we take seriously paragraph 37d of *Commitment to Mission and Unity* on p. 16 of the report. I quote it in full:

> Growth in fellowship
>
> Those sharing joint oversight would have a special responsibility to encourage the growth of fellowship in the following areas:
>
> (i) the sharing of worship;
>
> (ii) prayer for and with each other and the building up of a common life in mission and service;
>
> (iii) the extension of LEPs wherever Methodists and Anglicans live and worship in the same locality;
>
> (iv) the rationalisation of the use of buildings wherever Anglicans and Methodists live in close proximity;
>
> (v) closer co-operation in deaneries and circuits, together with the rationalisation of ecclesiastical boundaries to serve the mission of the Church;
>
> (vi) more effective deployment of ministers especially in rural areas and urban priority areas;
>
> (vii) the exchange of experience of women's ministry and of the experience of living with two recognised positions on the ordination of women to the presbyterate;
>
> (viii) joint processes of selection for ministry;
>
> (ix) increased provision for joint theological education for both lay and ordained;
>
> (x) joint decisions over who may be ordained, the appointment or stationing of ministers, matters of church property etc.

It is important for all the discussions to facilitate growth and development at the local level. This may well be an extension of LEPs and the co-operation of circuits and deaneries. This would surely make sense especially in rural areas and open up many creative possibilities. It is also possible to write large the philosophy of an LEP over a Diocese and District. This would involve commitment to strategic planning and the sharing of resources.

HOW CAN ALL THIS BE ENCOURAGED?

I suggest the following:

- The establishment of local covenants between clergy and/or churches. The beauty of a covenant is that it is free from bureaucracy and yet can be a real sign or signal to the community.
- Regular meetings between Methodist Local Preachers and Anglican Readers in the area and using Readers in Methodist Churches and Local Preachers in Anglican Churches as the Canon Law already permits with appropriate authorisation.
- Regular meetings between the clergy of a deanery and circuit (many are not co-terminus geographically but we must learn to be flexible at the 'edges') to enable planning of services.
- The creative use of buildings. Often the Church of England building is listed and sometimes without many facilities while the Methodist building can be used more flexibly. There are examples, e.g. Tickton near Beverley in Yorkshire, where the buildings are used in a complementary way.
- To encourage local churches to be involved together in local social issues and to encourage people to live on a large map by taking part in joint projects.
- To provide opportunities for the sharing of each other's spirituality, e.g. The Methodist Covenant Service and Easter vigils.
- For local congregations and clergy to prompt church leaders concerning their commitment and support for ecumenical ventures.
- For the Methodist Chairs/Chairmen and Anglican Bishops to meet in regions to form friendships and working relations.
- To create ecumenical areas over Circuits and Deaneries and District and Diocese.
- To explore the possibility of an ecumenical Bishop in a designated area.

The ecumenical movement provides us with many challenges and opportunities. It would be an easier course to opt out and to come to the conclusion that the problems are too difficult. Opting out is not on the agenda. The gospel demands us to seek a visible unity which in the end is a gift from God.

BIBLIOGRAPHY

Commitment to Mission and Unity (Church House and Methodist Publishing House), GS Misc 477.

Sharing in the Apostolic Commission (1996).

'Together in Mission and Ministry', *Porvoo Report* (Church House).

Called to be one (CTE Publication).

Together Locally, Jenny Carpenter.

Ut Unum Sint, Catholic Truth Society.

Anglican-Moravian Conversations, Council for Christian Unity.

Towards the making of an ecumenical Bishop in Wales, edited by Gethin Abraham Williams.

QUESTIONS

1 What is the theological basis for visible unity?

2 What experiences have you had — negative and positive — of working ecumenically?

3 Write down your hopes for the ecumenical movement in the 21st century and devise practical steps to make these a reality.

The Church and the Media

Moira Sleight

A CHARACTERISTIC of the late 20th century was the rapid growth and availability of methods of communication. This process will continue into the 21st century until there will be very few places in the world unreached by radio, television or the Internet. Alongside this there will be greatly increased choice and a gradual dismantling of restrictions on what people can see and hear in spite of Government attempts to prevent this. Satellite television and the Internet know no frontiers.

This will be both a curse and a blessing. The unpleasant aspects of human nature will have free rein but individuals will have access to information of every kind as never before. We must decide whether the proliferation of pornography is a price worth paying for access to libraries and resources around the globe and to documentaries of the highest quality.

This growth in the number and range of the means of mass communication is not the whole story. At the same time as the number of radio and television channels has increased, so has the dominance of a number of individuals who have built up large communication empires, often using their ownership of newspapers to promote their other media interests. Some of these individuals have not been content to run profitable businesses but have used their power to promote their own ideology. At the very least their media have been discouraged from reporting news which might adversely affect their proprietor's business interests in any part of the world.

This is nothing new in the world of newspapers. As one cynic commented: 'The freedom of the press is nothing more than the freedom of a newspaper proprietor to publish as many of his prejudices as the libel lawyers will allow.' In general the public recognises this and accepts that, despite C. P. Scott's claim that 'comment is free while facts are sacred', the line between fact and comment is sometimes blurred and the presentation of the news will reflect the general political and ideological line of the paper.

However, in the world of broadcasting, the public in Britain at least has different expectations due to the fact that radio and television developed under the control of a public body, the BBC, and that even when commercial television was introduced it operated within a structure which enshrined public service values and insisted on the objectivity and impartiality of its news output. New broadcasting channels do not have to respect the same public service ethos and it is by no means clear that their news services will be as free from proprietorial influence as are the BBC and the

ITV companies. This is a matter of concern to governments and Christian citizens will want to argue for a media policy which requires all broadcasters to respect the standards of objectivity to which we are accustomed.

Another area in which communication is a matter of political interest is protection of national culture. The dominance of the United States in the film industry has spread American culture throughout the world. Because of the size of the internal American market, films and television programmes can be exported and bought by other countries more cheaply than if they were to make the programmes themselves. This has been recognised not only as a benefit to American trade, as consumers are attracted to the lifestyle they see on the screen, but also as a way of spreading American political and social values. Many countries have seen this as a threat to their national culture and have taken steps to limit American influence, in some cases by the outright banning of imported films and television programmes, in others by the imposition of quotas. The matter has recently been perceived as even more urgent due to the increasing importance of audio visual resources in education. Are countries willing to pay the extra cost of generating their own resources or will education everywhere come more and more to reflect an American world view?

We use the term media to cover all forms of mass communication but there are important distinctions to be made between print media and broadcast media. The number and range of magazines, newspapers etc far exceeds the number and range of broadcast channels, particularly in the British Isles. Broadcast media are the more expensive and therefore access to using them is limited. The opportunities afforded to Christians to employ the mass media to communicate their message will therefore be different according to the medium.

There is a continuing discussion among Christians about the best ways to utilise the various media available. Almost all agree that the ownership of newspapers and magazines is appropriate for Christian bodies but few think this is appropriate for radio and television. Why is this?

Broadcasting is a one-way process. It is communication from the powerful to the powerless. The Christian message, on the other hand, must be communicated from the powerless to the powerful with opportunities for dialogue and response. Though some claim that radio and television are appropriate vehicles for evangelism, research into the ways in which people become Christians reveals that very few indeed are converted in response to a broadcast message. This is not to say, however, that Christians should not be involved in broadcasting.

The print medium, on the other hand, is comparatively inexpensive, can be used by virtually anyone — especially so in these days of desktop publishing — and affords easy opportunities for dialogue.

So, how can the Churches respond to the opportunities offered by the various forms of communication in ways that are appropriate and effective?

NATIONAL RADIO AND TELEVISION

Christian influence in this sphere is mainly exercised by talented individuals working in this area. For example, Methodist minister the Revd Dr Colin Morris was for many years head of religious broadcasting for the BBC and later BBC controller for Northern Ireland, while Baptist minister the Revd Steve Chalke is a popular presenter on both BBC and ITV.

Churches can play a role here by encouraging people with appropriate gifts to develop careers in broadcasting even if some regard that as a loss to the Church.

Christians should also be willing to write to programme makers with words of appreciation not just complaint.

LOCAL RADIO AND TELEVISION

Local broadcasting affords many more opportunities for direct involvement by individual Christians and churches. Care should be taken to cultivate a good relationship with the head of the local radio station and the news department of local radio and television stations. Many local radio stations broadcast community-based programmes which give a church an opportunity to explain itself to a wider constituency. However, it should not be thought that anyone can walk into a studio and perform well with a camera or microphone. Christians should seek opportunities for training. Contact your denomination's broadcasting or press officer for details.

CHRISTIAN BROADCASTING

In recent years there have been attempts to launch specifically Christian radio and television channels. One of the most successful has been London's Premier Radio. Opinions are divided over whether this is the right use of resources as on the whole only Christians listen to such stations whereas a Christian programme on a general channel is listened to by a cross-section of society.

NATIONAL PRESS

It is hard to find a major news story in the world today which does not have a religious dimension — for example, the conflicts in the Middle East, Africa and the Balkan states. Yet not all national newspapers employ qualified religious commentators and this is reflected in the covering of these stories. News about the churches rarely excites the interest of news editors unless it is a tale of an erring bishop or fisticuffs in a church council.

Churches try to place positive news stories through the efforts of their denominational press officers. These same officers also seek to minimise the damage caused by emerging scandals.

There is a limit to how local Christians can influence the national press, but one effective avenue is a well-phrased, concise letter on a topic of interest for the letters page. This method can also be used in response to anything that appears in the paper which calls for a Christian defence. However, time is of the essence and such a letter should be sent straight away.

LOCAL PRESS

In most cases local newspapers are understaffed and under-resourced and therefore receptive to well-written, properly presented, interesting articles about church affairs. Once again, care should be taken to build up a good relationship with the news editor and to research requirements and deadlines. The letters page of a local newspaper is even more open to individual Christians than a national publication and it is an avenue worth pursuing.

CHRISTIAN PRESS

Each denomination generates more news than the national press considers important for a general readership but the news is nevertheless important to members of that church. Thus there is a range of publications which seeks to serve either members of a particular denomination or certain wings of a number of churches. Often, as in the case of the *Methodist Recorder*, the newspapers are independent, taking neither finance nor interference from the church authorities.

The Christian press is used as a resource for the national media in that national religious correspondents will pick up stories from there. Local radio, in particular, follows up items first carried in the denominational weeklies.

Reading a denominational newspaper helps individual Christians have a non-parochial view. Learning about church matters on a national and international scale gives a breadth of understanding which helps them to live on a larger map.

In addition, reading a weekly newspaper of another denomination is an ideal way for ecumenically-minded Christians to keep in touch with what is concerning their fellow Christians in other churches.

All the religious press face the same difficulties in that membership of the churches is declining and therefore so is their potential readership. As papers try to reach out to new readers they are in danger of losing old readers who have come to like the present format. Evolution not revolution is often the key.

Denominational papers are entitled to ask for the support of members of their denomination as the papers can be a resource for study, training and mission. Individual members therefore should invite others to take the paper and see that their church has a contact person to encourage sales.

News items about local churches are always welcome, as is information about people with writing skills. Once again, the letters page is another arena for involvement.

SUMMARY

In general we have seen two ways in which modern developments present challenges and opportunities to Christians and to churches. The first is the opportunity to become involved in the communication process. Opportunities will be greatest at local level but the church must be willing to support those with the appropriate gifts to play their part at every level. With the exception of denominational newspapers, where Christian ownership is obviously appropriate, our aim should be to contribute to the media, sharing ideas and experiences and encouraging the media to reflect the whole of our common life together.

The second is the need to engage with governments in devising a strategy for the media which allows the greatest possible freedom in the flow of ideas, which protects the best features of the nation's identity and within which the media may enhance the quality of life of all its citizens.

QUESTIONS

1 Is the proportion of British films in our cinemas or British programming on our television screens about right? If not, what changes would be desirable and how could they be brought about?

2 List the television and radio programmes you think are (a) particularly effective (b) particularly ineffective in communicating a Christian message. Give reasons.

3 What attention does your local radio station give to religion? Can you improve this in some way?

4 Should the churches own television or radio stations or would the resources be better used elsewhere?

5 Have there been items in the national secular press this week which have ignored or misrepresented a Christian point of view? Discuss these and write a letter to the editor.

6 Does your local church have a media officer? What can you do to raise the profile of your church and its concerns?

7 What suggestions can you make for developing your denominational newspaper?

Freedom Through Justice

Rachel Backhurst

> Is not this the kind of fasting I have chosen: to loose the chains of injustice and untie the cords of the yoke, to set the oppressed free and break every yoke? Is it not to share your food with the hungry and to provide the poor wanderer with shelter — when you see the naked, to clothe him, and not to turn away from your own flesh and blood?
> Isaiah 58:6–7

I STRUGGLE to live in a world where over 80% of wealth is shared by just 20% of its population. I struggle not because I wake every day asking myself where the food will come from to feed my family, or whether the water I walk miles to collect will be life or death to my children. I struggle because I live in the knowledge that I am one of the 20%. There is a proverb: 'There is plenty of food in the fallow fields of the poor. It is the lack of justice that causes the waste.' I believe we are all called to loose the chains of injustice, and to release the food, creativity, hopes and dreams that lie in the fallow fields of the poor. It is not charity to do so, but a shared responsibility and a commitment to justice.

We live in a world where millions are trapped by debt and exploitation; where 1.3 billion people live in absolute poverty, that is on less than 60p a day; where rich nations take back £9 in debt repayments for every £1 given in aid; where the top ten supermarkets ring up an annual turnover equal to the income of the 35 poorest developing countries; and where a child dies of hunger every eight seconds.

Extreme poverty affects us all, not only on a humanitarian and moral level, but in our whole world system. We live in an inter-dependent world where we cannot close our eyes and pretend a problem does not affect us. To escape poverty, the rainforests are being cut down for desperately needed cash whilst damaging our environment, and likewise, drugs are being increasingly grown as cash crops to release on the international market. To quote Lilla Watson, an Australian Aboriginal leader: 'If you have come to help me, you are wasting your time. But if you have come because your liberation is bound up with mine, then let us walk together.' At the turn of the millennium the message has never been so clear, that there is a need for justice, a need to walk together, and a need for freedom from poverty.

Behind the injustice of a widening gap between rich and poor lie issues of trade, development and power, as poverty is exploited instead of eradicated. One such exploitation which has now reached crisis point is the problem of debt. To give a brief history of this crisis, developing countries began borrowing substantial amounts of money in the 1970s. Interest rates were low at this time, even negative at one point, and commercial banks flush with oil money strongly encouraged borrowing. Unfortunately in the early 1980s new economic policies in the West made world interest rates rise dramatically. At the same time the prices of raw materials exported by poor countries fell sharply. With these soaring interest rates and decreased income from their exports poor countries, unable to make ends meet, turned to the wealthy governments and international financial institutions who offered new loans to help repay old ones. A vicious, inescapable spiral began.

In the UK we have bankruptcy proceedings to limit the damaging consequences of unpayable debts. Unfortunately there is no international bankruptcy law, and despite poor countries having paid back two or three times what they originally borrowed, the debt is still growing as it is passed on from generation to generation. It is not simply the existence of the debt that leads to the problem. Many countries have huge international debts, including the USA. However, in many of the world's poorest countries, debt repayments to rich countries and international financial institutions have to take priority over the lives and prospects of millions of people. These countries' debts have grown so large that the interest payments alone often amount to more than they can afford to spend on health care and education combined. Poor countries are spending money on servicing their debt repayments at the expense of their peoples' health, education, clean water and sanitation.

In Mozambique, where only a third of the population have access to safe drinking water and adult literacy is little higher, 33% of public expenditure is spent on debt service, while education gets only 7.9%, and health a mere 3.3%. Mozambique's debt stands at around $111 billion while the annual earnings per person stand at $90. Debt is an immediate human problem, with the poorest paying quite literally with their lives. As more than two million people die each year from effects of unsafe, polluted water, and 2.5 million unvaccinated children die each year from measles, tetanus and whooping cough, money that should be being spent on the people is diverted into debt repayments.

There is a biblical response to this crisis. The principle of Jubilee, found in Leviticus 25, aimed to restore justice and fairness to societies which had fallen short of God's ideal. It called on people to celebrate every 50 years with the cancellation of debts, the return of land to its original owners and the freeing of slaves. The aim was to encourage a new start, with better economic systems and fairer ways of living, so that next time around injustice would not creep in so readily. The idea was never fully embraced, but it is still there to inspire us. As we celebrate 2000 years since the birth of Christ, we have an opportunity through this God-given idea to give a new start to millions of people.

A diverse grouping of organisations across the world is calling for a one-off act of Jubilee: the cancellation of poor countries' unpayable debts. The Jubilee 2000 Coalition (consisting of development agencies, church groups, trade unions and community groups) believes these debts should be reduced so that countries can allocate more of their resources to combating poverty and developing their economies. This would mean the poor could start the millennium with hope and real opportunity, rather than struggling under a burden from which they can never escape.

There is also a degree to which lenders should take some responsibility for the reckless way some loans were made. Loans were often given to prop up politically useful dictators and to promote western business interests abroad. Indeed 95% of loans made by Britain were to encourage countries to buy our own exports, especially arms. At present it is only the debtors who are paying for this. And how much would it cost? Jubilee 2000 proposes a realistic debt relief package; enough to enable poor countries to find a lasting route out of their poverty. Christian Aid, one of the coalition members, believes this will mean cancelling just over £100 billion of debt. This seems a lot, but in proportion to the amount of money circulating in the world economy it is relatively small. The daily turnover of the world currency markets is more than ten times this amount, and it is equivalent to what the USA spends on going to the cinema in just one year. The money spent on chocolate in the UK in one year would clear African debt to the UK in one go.

The prospect of debt relief is not unprecedented. Germany enjoyed debt relief following the Second World War that was far more generous than that currently being requested for the poorest countries today. Its economy is now one of the strongest in the world. A similar vision and enlightened economic approach is required to that of the Marshall Plan that rebuilt Europe after the Second World War. Corporations are also being given preferential treatment, for example, Eurodisney incurred losses of £860 million in just two years and received generous treatment from creditors.

Of course freedom from debt is not the same as freedom from poverty (although unless there is substantial debt cancellation, progress for many countries will be impossible). There are many problems at the heart of the gap between rich and poor. Uganda is an unfortunate example of this. It is one of the few countries to have received some relief on its unpayable debts. However, following this, the price of coffee on the international market fell sharply. Developing countries are heavily dependent on their cash crops (often through following Western creditors' advice to try and boost their exports in order to service their debt) and Uganda is no exception. This meant disaster for the country, and its situation is almost back to what it was before experiencing debt relief. There is a need to think about our whole trade system, as wealth continues to flow from the poor to the rich.

We are living in an increasingly global market, where goods are available in our shops from all over the world, and increasingly from developing countries. Poverty is often exploited to provide cheap labour, materials and products in the area of trade. This unfair trade stems from the huge power the West holds over producers desperate for cash. Producers are often paid a few pence for products that sell for pounds in our shops, whilst working in punishing working conditions, with lack of social or legal protection, and denial of workers' rights to freedom of speech and organisation. There has been increasing consumer pressure for this to change. Here again the solution lies in justice.

I work for a fair trade company called 'And Albert'. We trade mainly in crafts and furnishings from developing countries and our inspiration is the Isaiah passage above. We seek to be an economic expression of the principles of justice, compassion and creativity, which lie at the heart of the Judaeo-Christian ethic. Seeking out the poorest, most oppressed communities in the world we aim, through personal relationship, to create a consistent, ongoing partnership of trust. We offer a fair price with advance payment. Our trading partnerships stimulate work in a community and promote sustainable economic justice. We want to see human rights restored, creativity released and the contrasting colour of different cultures celebrated. These principles are foundational for ethical business, yet lie in stark contrast to much business practice in the West. We also pledge to share a proportion of our sales revenue and profits with our overseas partnerships, empowering them to develop their own education, health care and local economies. This works as a two-way process. The richness of their creativity is the key to our business strategy. This is not charity, but fairness. We hope to show a business model which genuinely ends the injustice that a system based purely on consumer driven capitalism has produced.

There is such dignity to give through fair trade, and hope, as it becomes more widely known and recognised. 'And Albert' should not be the unique and alternative business that it is. Fair payment and decent working conditions should be a right, not a luxury; just practice, not charity. We are a working model of a just trading system, and it can work. We are calling for freedom from unfair trade, freedom from exploitation, freedom from debt. A freedom not through charity, but through justice.

> At the end of our life we will not be judged by how many diplomas we have received, how much money we have made, how many great things we have done. We will be judged by: I was hungry and you gave me food to eat, I was naked and you clothed me, I was homeless and you took me in. Hungry not only for bread, but hungry for love, naked not only of clothing but of human dignity and respect, homeless not only for a room of bricks but homeless because of rejection.
>
> Mother Teresa

QUESTIONS

1 Why is the idea of Jubilee so difficult to embrace?

2 How might we move from charity to justice?

3 Should any conditions be placed on debt relief?

4 Consider what you have eaten, worn and used today. On whom have you been dependent? Who might you have unfairly exploited?

5 Share practical ideas of how individuals, groups and churches might address the issue of fair trade.

The Human City

David Clark

As THE Christian Church, and not least Methodism, struggles to identify its place within an increasingly pluralistic and materialistic society, it could do a great deal worse than look at what Christian faith has to contribute to a new vision for 'the city' in the millennium before us. As religious language appears to many ever more archaic in a post-modern society, 'the city' remains at least one concept which still connects the world of the sacred and the world of the secular.

But the world of the secular is now struggling with the nature of the city. It knows, for better or for worse, that the city will shape the future of civilisation. By the turn of the century half the world's population will be living in cities. The new millennium will require places where more and more people can come together to live, to learn, to work, and to play. The village and the neighbourhood will remain important; the region will have increasing significance; 'the world is (now) our parish'. But it is the city — not too small to be claustrophobic nor too vast to be completely anonymous — which many believe holds the key to being the most significant communal focus for the future of humankind.

'REDEEMING THE CITY'

It is not surprising, therefore, that we are now experiencing a multitude of endeavours to 'redeem the city'. It is by no means yet what we would want it to be. Witness the campaigns for 'the sustainable city', 'the safe city', 'the healthy city', 'the learning city'... And no wonder. For it now has to be all hands on deck. Unless the public, the private (still a very reluctant partner) and the voluntary sectors all play their part, our expanding cities will simply explode and collapse.

So far, however, one key word has failed to appear in the vast literature describing our vision for the city in the next millennium: that of 'the human city'. This is strange because, as we have discovered here in Birmingham and describe below, it is the dehumanising nature of contemporary institutions as they are driven by the increasingly inhuman aspects of a competitive economy, which depresses, disempowers and infuriates people. It is not so much the inevitable upsets of modern urban life — frequent change of job, the stress of a new pace to living, loss of support from the extended family — which destroy morale, but the inhumanity of those institutions with which people have to deal as a result of such pressures.

If our world is to survive and flourish in the millennium on the horizon it needs, above all, 'the *human* city'. We will simply not make it through another thousand years if the wealth creators ignore human wealth creation, if 'the included' refuse to identify and share with 'the excluded' and if the city transforms itself physically and materially but loses its soul in the process.

'THE HUMAN CITY INSTITUTE'

In the summer of 1997 a unique association came into being in Birmingham. The Human City Institute is a consortium of over thirty Birmingham organisations representing Christian, other faith and secular bodies, as well as the voluntary, public and private sectors. The Birmingham Methodist District is amongst its members. The Institute's purpose is 'to enable those who share a vision of Birmingham as a human city to work together with others to make that vision a reality'. The Human City Institute sprang out of an initiative taken in 1995 by Westhill College of Higher Education, a Free Church foundation and member of the Selly Oak Colleges Federation, to seek to put its mission statement into action more practically on the Birmingham scene. The first two years of this initiative concentrated mainly on networking lay members of the Christian churches across the city to encourage them to move the issue of the humanity of the places where they lived or worked much higher up the agenda of their neighbourhood or organisation. As more and more people from beyond the churches were drawn in, the decision was taken to set up the Human City Institute as a body open to all committed to a vision of Birmingham as a human city.

Since its establishment in 1997, the Institute has focused its efforts on four main activities:

- publishing a *Human City Bulletin*, carrying news and views about Birmingham as a human city, now going out to some 2500 people;
- holding a series of ten public 'hearings' in Birmingham's Council House on the theme of *Imagine Birmingham*, attended by some 500 people. At these hearings leading figures in the life of the city led sessions on such topics as: *Imagine a human education system; Imagine a human police force; Imagine a human business world; Imagine a human transport system* ... These hearings have helped to form an ongoing agenda for the Human City Institute;
- setting up a city-wide network of *human city sites*, groups from all sectors and of all sizes which for up to one year commit themselves to fulfil a publicly declared human agenda of their own choosing and to co-operate with other sites in the process;

- working for the establishment of human city sites across a number of disadvantaged neighbourhoods within Birmingham, a project now being extended to Bradford and Swindon.

The Human City Institute is only at the very beginning of a long and demanding journey of discovery in search of the holy grail! For at the heart of the endeavour lies the ultimate question, 'What *is* a human city?'

THE QUEST FOR THE HUMAN — A SHARED ENDEAVOUR

Paradoxical as it may seem, the power of the idea of 'the human city' comes from the fact that only we as citizens can envision and earth it. There will, of course, always be those who dwell on the downside of human nature pointing with some satisfaction (because it lets all of us off the hook) to the many personal and corporate failures of urban life as 'only human'. But far more people, as the citizens of Birmingham have shown, want to see the human city as one embracing the very best that human beings can offer. Set out in the box below are the signs of such a city which we have discerned so far.

We believe that the impetus for change comes not from the pessimists but from those who want to enter into the debate about the enormous potential of every citizen and every sector of urban life to share in enriching their part of the human city — be that the human street, the human school, the human hospital, the human business, the human city centre or a human system of local government, not to mention the human mosque, the human temple or (dare we who call ourselves Christians face it) the human church!

When the vision of the human city becomes the focal point of civic renewal, individuals and organisations representing every aspect of urban life are enabled to share their vision and work together in new and creative ways to make that vision a reality — not least the church. For Christian faith down the ages has, often at great cost, learnt an immense amount about the reality of human nature; not only about how to deal with its darkest features, but how to celebrate 'the glory of man' which in turn bears witness to 'the glory of God', as Irenaeus once put it.

CHRISTIANS IN THE THICK OF THINGS

Christians believe that human beings really were created in the image of God. Despite the appalling consequences of evil, witnessed again and again in the squalor, corruption and violence of every city, human beings have, therefore, been given the power to create great and glorious cities. After all, their final destination is a 'new Jerusalem'. And, as Evelyn Underhill wrote half a century ago, 'Creation is the activity of the artist possessed by the vision of perfection'.

It is to this God-given human potential that Christians are called to bear witness in our civilisation's city building of the future. A church which is prepared to risk mixing with those of all faiths and none in the task of creating the human city will find that it is not simply being asked to provide plant and skills and pastoral know-how, however important those may be. It will discover, perhaps to its amazement, that it is again being called upon to help give the city a soul, and to tell once more the story of a God of unbounded compassion who has the resources to help human beings make all things new, even cities.

TEN SIGNS OF A HUMAN CITY

Since the Human City Institute got underway, it has discerned a number of recurring themes which are set out here as signs of a human city: as well as of a human neighbourhood, school, hospital, business, police force, system of local government... *For the humanity of the part and the humanity of the whole are essential and complementary.*

A human city is committed to being a new kind of city. A human city is committed to the city as a place alive with the energy of hope, to the city which enables imagination and creativity to flourish, to the city which offers opportunities for people to care and share, to the city as a community of communities which brings a powerful sense of solidarity, to the city which celebrates achievements of every kind.

A human city is about '*value for people*' before value for money. It treasures diversity and difference. It is where '*all matter and each counts*'. It is a place where people acknowledge and affirm one another. It is a friendly and nurturing city, a city with a human face.

A human city gives life to its citizens. That means safe, clean and healthy surroundings. But it also means that such cities are places of beauty and grace; places to which people want to return. The human city provides an environment wherein one can celebrate the past, relish the present and get excited about the future.

A human city knows the suffering inhumanity causes. It recognises the cost of confronting the forces that dehumanise. But it remains committed to the vision of a just and inclusive city and works to make such a vision a reality.

A human city is about *human* wealth creation. It draws on the total experience of all its citizens: body, mind and spirit. It has a heart and a soul. A human city believes in the importance of the ordinary human experiences of its citizens. It is a city where *small* (and not just the great) *is beautiful.*

A human city is about openness and trust built on truth and honesty. It is about straight communication.

No city can thrive whose citizens are passive and apathetic. A human city is committed to giving a voice to its citizens whilst enabling them to take responsibility for their own destinies.

A human city values those connections which join sectors (public, private and voluntary), neighbourhoods, cultures and generations in new and creative ways. In a human city it is always '*better together*'. But a human city also recognises the cost of genuine partnership; it knows that for genuine partnership to develop, trust, commitment, tolerance, forgiveness and reconciliation will always be needed. A human city is a listening city. It is a city which creates safe spaces for transforming dialogue, quiet reflection and the birth of new understandings. If offers an education for life. A human city is about fundamental and continuing change; structurally and organisationally as well as individually. A human city is never afraid to take big risks to discover how to make life more human for its citizens.

QUESTIONS

1 'The glory of God is man fully alive' (Irenaeus). Do you agree?

2 From the signs of a human city set out in the box choose the one which you feel is the most important (or add your own 'most important' sign if necessary). Compare the group's different choices. How can you make your chosen sign more of a reality where you live or work?

3 What does it mean to be a human church? How could your local church be made more human ? What are you going to do to help this happen?

Material about the Human City Institute and its work can be obtained from The Human City Institute, Westhill College, Selly Oak, Birmingham B29 6LL.

Tel: 0121 472 7245 Web site: http://www@humancity.org

Postscript

I am grateful to all those who have contributed to this book. You may not have agreed with what has been written but I hope the essays will stimulate thinking.

Of course, other topics could and perhaps should have been included. The list is endless. Yet hopefully the essays will provoke thinking for individuals and discussion for housegroups. Over to you!

ACKNOWLEDGMENTS

To Pat Wass for collating the scripts and to Graham Jones for proof reading.

Editor

Contributors

RACHEL BACKHURST
Fairtrade Shop Manager and Chair of the York Christian Aid Action Group

MARK BENNETT
IT Consultant

BERNARD BRADY
Psychotherapist in Nottingham

STUART J. BURGESS
President of the Methodist Conference

DAVID CLARK
Methodist Minister
Co-ordinator of the Human City Institute
Westhill College, Birmingham

HAROLD S. CLARK
Methodist Minister
Director, Mission in Business Industry & Commerce
Harpenden

ARTHUR FAIRHURST
Retired Senior Executive, Chemical Industry

ANNE KRISMAN
Head of RE, teaching pupils with general learning difficulties, in a special school in Redbridge, and a member of the South West Essex Settlement and Reform synagogue

CATHY MICHELL
Head of Religious Studies
Hills Road Sixth Form College, Cambridge

GEORGINA MORLEY
Director of Studies
NE Oecumenical Course

LESLIE MORLEY
Rector of St Peter's, Nottingham

JULIE NORRIS
Methodist Minister
Cambridge

JENI PARSONS
Team Vicar
Worcester

ANTHONY REDDIE
Birmingham Initiative in Christian Education

HELEN REID
Faith to Faith Project, Touchstone, Bradford

WALTER SCHENK
Methodist Minister
Board of Global Ministries, New York

MOIRA SLEIGHT
Editor, *The Methodist Recorder*

CATHERINE WELLS
Methodist Youth President 1999

MERVYN WILLSHAW
Chairman, London South West District of the Methodist Church